United States
Department of
Agriculture

Forest Service

Southern
Research Station

General Technical
Report SRS–114

Documentation and User Guides for SPBLOB: A Computer Simulation Model of the Joint Population Dynamics for Loblolly Pine and the Southern Pine Beetle

John Bishir, James Roberds, Brian Strom, and Xiaohai Wan

I0435961

The Authors:

John Bishir, Professor Emeritus, Department of Mathematics, North Carolina State University, Raleigh, NC 27695-8205; **James Roberds**, Research Geneticist, (retired) Southern Institute of Forest Genetics, U.S. Forest Service, Southern Research Station, Saucier, MS 39574; **Brian Strom**, Research Entomologist, U.S. Forest Service, Southern Research Station, Research Unit on Insects, Diseases and Invasive Plants, Pineville, LA 71360; and **Xiaohai (Robert) Wan**, Research Scientist, Eli Lilly and Company, Lilly Corporate Center, Indianapolis, IN 46285.

Disclaimers Associated with SPBLOB Itself

We consider the **SPBLOB** model and its accompanying simulation code primarily as research tools, rather than accurate predictors of stand timber volume or degree of beetle activity in *particular* stand scenarios. The reason is that fundamental beetle activities—egg production, development in juvenile stages, movement, and mortality—are controlled largely by temperature (Coulson 1980, Payne 1980, Stephen and Lih 1985, Ungerer and others 1999, Wagner and others 1984a, Wagner and others 1984b), which, in turn, is subject to unpredictable chance fluctuations. In addition, field observations indicate that in some stands beetles appear in considerable numbers (e.g., via migration from outside) by age 10 or before, while others remain free of beetle infestations throughout their existence. Thus, model comparisons of management strategies (e.g., clonal plantings vs. those generated from seedlings or, in clonally generated stands, block plantings vs. random mix of ramets) should be based, not on single stand simulations, but rather on multiple, independent replications (we suggest 200 or more) of any potential strategies.

No model is perfect or complete in the sense that no model can include all the subtle details and interactions that exist in a real system. Our model simulates the joint dynamics of southern pine beetles and loblolly pines. We particularly focus on tree growth, because it allows prediction of timber volume (Burkhart and others 1987), and on oleoresin flow rates because "the oleoresin system in pines is the primary defensive mechanism against attack by bark beetles" (Blanche and others 1983). We do not include beetle competitors or predators, nor do we consider effects on trees of important pathogens introduced by attacking beetles. We also omit a variety of mechanisms, such as 'hypersensitive' lesion formation in response to fungi (Berryman 1972) and growth/differentiation balance (Lorio 1986, Lorio and others 1990), thought by some investigators to be factors in host defense against bark beetle attack. In the future, the latter may be incorporated as an environmental adjustment to oleoresin yield.

Estimates of important model parameters vary in the literature so we have had to choose among them. Some processes and parameters included in the model and its simulation code have not, as far as we know, been studied quantitatively. For these we have assigned parameter values that result in code output that approximates observed stand outcomes, in particular, the qualitative behavior of beetles and the tree mortality they cause.

While this code has been extensively tested and checked against results of field studies reported in the literature, neither the Forest Service, U.S. Department of Agriculture nor the authors accept responsibility for errors or inaccuracies that arise. We provide absolutely no warranty of any kind, either expressed or implied, including but not limited to, warranties of merchantability or fitness for a particular purpose.

January 2009

Southern Research Station
200 W.T. Weaver Blvd.
Asheville, NC 28804

Documentation and User Guides for SPBLOB: A Computer Simulation Model of the Joint Population Dynamics for Loblolly Pine and the Southern Pine Beetle

John Bishir, James Roberds, Brian Strom,
and Xiaohai Wan

Preface

This publication describes and documents **SPBLOB**, a computer simulation model for initiation, expansion, and decline of southern pine beetle (SPB: *Dendroctonus frontalis* Zimm.) infestations in loblolly pine (*Pinus taeda* L.) plantations from time of stand establishment until harvest. The model code also simulates planting, growth, and mortality of each tree in the stand. This documentation includes four major components:

- **Documentation** for **SPBLOB**, which provides information about the code structure and the values for the parameters contained in the **SPBLOB** code

- Two **User Guides** that explain the choices available in setting up stand simulations, together with interpretation of simulation output

- A **Glossary** that lists and defines the constants, variables, and parameters used in the simulation code

- **Literature Citations** for articles and books that contributed information upon which **SPBLOB** model structure and the major code parameter values are based

The **Source Code** for **SPBLOB,** and two **Executable Versions**—one for specifying and running single simulations, the other for multiple independent simulations—can be downloaded from **www.srs.fs.usda.gov/idip/**. Updated information about links will be available from the authors. While this code has been extensively tested and checked against results of field studies reported in the literature, undetected errors no doubt exist. We will be most grateful to users who inform us of these.

Legalities

The compilers, random number generators, and command files used in connection with the **SPBLOB** code have been downloaded from sites in the public domain. Citations and credits appear as appropriate in **chapter VI** of this documentation. More detailed information, including disclaimers and legal requirements associated with these uses, is contained in **appendix B**.

Acknowledgments

Development of this model was supported by grants provided by the Southern Institute of Forest Genetics, Southern Research Station, U.S. Forest Service, Saucier, MS, and by the Southern Research Station, Insects, Diseases, and Invasive Plants, U.S. Forest Service, Pineville, LA.

Our special thanks go to professor **Harold Burkhart**, Department of Forestry, Virginia Polytechnic Institute and State University (VPI), and his colleagues at VPI and the Westvaco Corporation, Summerville, SC, who generously allowed us to include parts of **PTAEDA2**, their simulation code for competitive tree growth and mortality (Burkhart and others 1987, Daniels and Burkhart 1975).

We also thank **James Meeker**, U.S. Forest Service, Southern Region Forest Health Protection, who graciously provided us much useful information pertaining to southern pine beetle behavior.

CONTENTS

ABSTRACT

SPBLOB is a computer simulation model for the interaction between loblolly pine (*Pinus taeda* L.), the economically most important forest crop in the United States, and the southern pine beetle (SPB: *Dendroctonus frontalis* Zimm.), the major insect pest for this species. The model simulates loblolly pine stands from time of planting until harvest. It mimics day-to-day changes in SPB populations, and the associated tree mortality caused by these bark beetles. In addition, it provides yearly updates of tree mortality due to competition and of growth for the surviving trees. Chiefly, the model and its simulation codes are designed to function as research tools for investigating the influence of stand properties on SPB activities, and of the reciprocal impact of beetles on tree mortality.

Model output relates to both trees and beetles. Simulations provide daily and yearly fluctuations in the size, composition, and spread of beetle populations within a stand. Stand types (e.g., plantations derived from seedlings or from clonally generated materials) can be compared in terms of average total merchantable volume of timber per acre at time of harvest and/or by average proportions of surviving trees. Average stand yields in the presence of beetles can also be compared with those when beetles are absent, thus providing a basis for estimating the real cost of beetle damage in loblolly stands.

In this **Documentation** we briefly describe the model, then outline the concepts and structure upon which the **SPBLOB** simulation source code is based. The included **User Guides** specify the input information regarding a loblolly stand and its environment required to run two executable **Simulation Codes**—a single-stand **Interactive Simulation** code, in which a user can specify features they wish the simulated stand to possess, and a **Multiple-Simulation** code that can be used to run large numbers of independent replicates of various stand designs. These **Guides** also describe the extensive variety of information about simulated tree and beetle populations that can be retrieved during simulations.

Keywords: Clonal plantation, *Dendroctonus frontalis*, merchantable volume, oleoresin flow, *Pinus taeda*, population dynamics, simulation model.

I. INTRODUCTION

This report documents and provides user guides for the computer simulation model **SPBLOB**, a model of the joint population dynamics between loblolly pine and the southern pine beetle (SPB) over the entire life of a stand. Loblolly pine (*Pinus taeda* L.) is the leading commercial timber species in the United States, growing on more than 13.4 million hectares (Schultz 1997). Southern pine beetle (SPB: *Dendroctonus frontalis* Zimm.) is the most destructive insect pest of pine forests in the Southeastern United States. Although SPB attacks all pine species within its range (Payne 1980), loblolly pine is its major host.

The **SPBLOB** model tracks day-to-day changes in beetle populations on and in each tree in a stand, as well as the tree mortality caused by beetle attacks. In addition, it provides yearly updates of tree growth and mortality associated with intrastand competition and lightning. Other models and simulation packages for projecting SPB dynamics exist (Coulson and others 1989, Lih and others 1995, Stephen and Lih 1985). However, these are primarily 'single season' models, focusing on 'spot growth,' the rapid increase and spread of SPB that periodically occurs when beetle populations reach critical mass. Beetle populations wax and wane in our model as well, and spots occur, these being driven by the fundamental, underlying time-varying interactions of temperature, numbers of beetles at different levels of maturity, and individual tree locations and their susceptibility to beetle attack.

Chapter II gives a brief description of the overall structure of the model code, including the purpose and output of each of its subroutines.

The **Source Code** for model simulation can be downloaded from **www.srs.fs.usda.gov/idip/**. This download package also includes:

- An electronic copy of this **Documentation**
- Other materials explaining the **SPBLOB** model and code
- Two **Executable Versions** of this code

The first executable version is an **Interactive** code that enables a user to specify a desired stand setup, and to run individual simulations of that stand. The second executable code runs **Multiple Independent Simulations** of any of 23 different stand scenarios, each by entering a single command. Chapters III and IV serve as respective **User Guides** for these executable codes.

Following the **User Guides**, chapters V, VI, and VII contain, respectively, detailed information concerning the values and literature sources for the most important **parameters** in the model; a list of **Literature Cited** in this **Documentation**; and a **Glossary** of principal variables and parameters that appear in the source code.

II. THE MODEL AND ITS SIMULATION CODE

A. Introduction

This chapter provides an overview of the **SPBLOB** source code, including a descriptive summary of each of the major subroutines. A more detailed discussion appears in chapter V, which explains the principal computations in the code, along with the major parameters, their values, and their sources in the literature.

Briefly, **SPBLOB** is a computer simulation model of the joint population dynamics between loblolly pine and the SPB. Our original impetus for developing this model was to evaluate deployment patterns of clonally generated tree materials. Our goal was to determine the pattern—individual clonal blocks or a random mixture of trees from all clones—that produces, on average, the greatest amount of merchantable timber from a stand (see, e.g., Bishir and Roberds 1999, Muhs 1993, Roberds and Bishir 1997, Roberds and others 1990). The nature of this question requires knowledge of individual tree attributes and their effects on beetle populations. Thus, we settled on a model that is discrete in:

- **Space**—Each tree is a separate entity, its interactions with its neighbors being affected by distances to them and by its size relative to theirs
- **Population size**—Trees and beetles can be counted, and individuals of each species react to their own immediate surroundings
- **Time**—There are yearly updates of the growth of surviving stems and of tree mortality due to competition

During each year, the model tracks day-to-day changes in the beetle numbers at each tree, and the resulting tree mortality they cause.

The flexibility of this structure allows the model code to simulate joint loblolly/SPB population dynamics over the entire life of a stand. (There is no practical limit on stand lifetime; see section III.B.1 for details.) In this generality, the model is capable of application to any loblolly stand, ranging from natural stands to commercial plantings, together with any level of beetle populations.

This having been said, we consider the model and its accompanying simulation code primarily as research tools, rather than accurate predictors of stand timber volume or the degree of beetle activity in *particular* stand scenarios. The reason is that primary beetle activities—egg production, development in juvenile stages, movement, and mortality—are controlled largely by temperature (Coulson 1980, Payne 1980, Stephen and Lih 1985, Ungerer and others 1999, Wagner and others 1984a, Wagner and others 1984b), which, in turn, is subject to unpredictable chance fluctuations. In addition, field observations indicate that in some stands beetles can appear in considerable numbers (e.g., via migration from outside) by age 10 or before, while others remain free of beetle infestations throughout their existence. Thus, model comparisons of management strategies (e.g., clonal plantings vs. those generated from seedlings or, in clonally generated stands, block plantings vs. random mix of ramets) should not be based on single stand simulations, but rather on multiple, independent replications of any proposed strategy. (Because of the wide variation among results of different simulations, we recommend running 200 or more simulations of each stand scenario studied; see chapter IV for further detail.)

Model computations relating to SPB focus almost entirely on females because they alone oviposit and they, not males, select host trees. In the model code, males play only one significant role, the production of repelling pheromone that leads to termination of attack (section E.5.5). Otherwise, all beetle population categories and beetle activities described pertain solely to the female portion of the population.

For convenience, the description that follows concerns commercial loblolly pine plantations; minor modifications are required for natural stands. Simulated stands are subject to beetle infestation. However, if desired, a user can specify a 'no-beetle' option. In this case, the code is a modified version of the tree growth simulator **PTAEDA2** developed by Daniels and Burkhart (1975) and Burkhart and others (1987).

B. Overview

The source code for **SPBLOB** is written in Fortran, a Windows-based version of which can be downloaded from **www.srs.fs.usda.gov/idip/**. Executable versions of this code are also available at this site. These executable codes are discussed in chapters III and IV.

Each stand simulation consists of five stages:

- Choosing tree materials and planting the stand at the desired density
- Tree growth and survival through an 8-year juvenile period in which no beetles are present
- Subsequent daily updates of the numbers of beetles at each tree, and the tree mortality they cause
- Yearly updates of tree growth and mortality related to tree competition
- Timber harvest

Figure 1 shows the relationships among the source code subroutines. Initially, program flow is governed by subroutine **MAIN** which, in subroutines **NOCLONE** through **CORRELATE** (read left to right in the top level of the figure), translates user specifications into a particular stand to be simulated. Subroutine **JUVEN** then projects stand growth and survival through an 8-year juvenile period during which no beetles are present, after which subroutine **PARBTL** assigns the parameters that govern beetle vital rates. At this point control passes to subroutine **SIMUL**, which directs traffic for the remainder of the simulation (second and third levels of the figure).

Under **SIMUL**, there are:

- Yearly updates by routines **OUTPUT, COMP2,** and **GROW2** of tree growth and survival related to intrastand competition
- Yearly reinitialization in subroutine **BEGYR** of tree resin flow rates and some beetle-related counts
- Lightning strikes simulated daily by subroutine **LIGHTNING**
- Daily changes in beetle populations on individual trees due to beetle mortality, oviposition, and juvenile maturation, computed in subroutines **TEMP** through **DISPERSE**

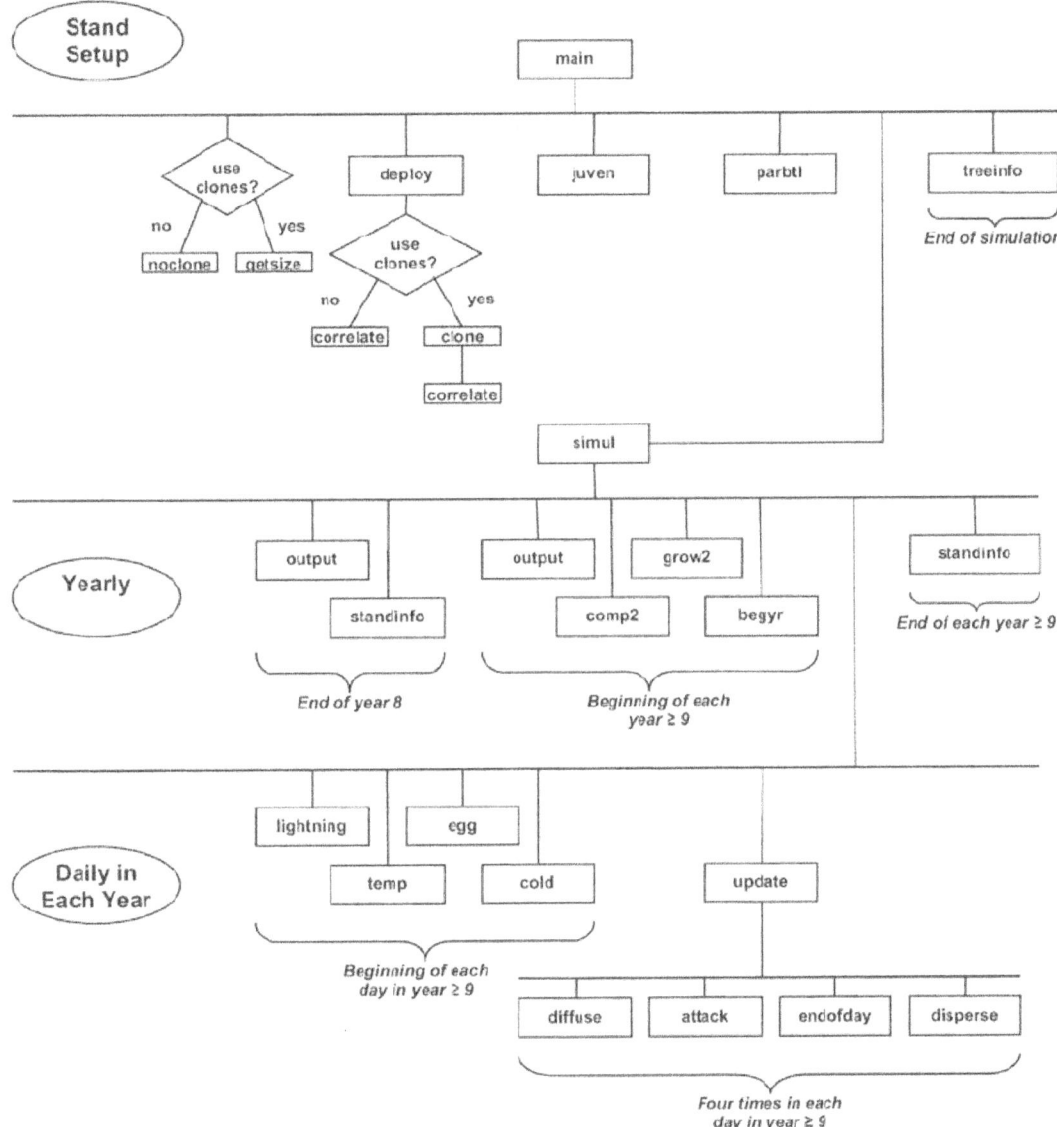

Figure 1—Flow diagram for source code subroutines.

- Yearly end-of-season summaries of stand status contained in subroutine **STANDINFO**

- Merchantable timber at harvest approximated by subroutine **OUTPUT**

- Summary information about each planted tree recorded at harvest time by subroutine **TREEINFO**

In the remainder of chapter II we focus on the *structure* of the code, including the purposes and outputs of the individual subroutines. Chapter V can be consulted for information about the principal code parameters, their numerical values, and their literature sources.

C. Plantation Establishment

C.1. Setting the Stand Parameters—Subroutine MAIN

C.2. Choosing Tree Materials—Subroutines NOCLONE, CLONE, and DEPLOY

Planting occurs in stages that correspond to major management decisions underlying stand establishment:

- Assignment of overall stand parameters
- Choice of materials to be planted and the pattern in which to plant them
- Planting of the chosen materials

This subroutine allows users to specify values of individual parameters (chapter III) or to choose an entire parameter group from a prescribed list of parameters (chapter IV) that among them determine stand geometry and harvest age, beetle vital rates, and relevant environmental quantities. Major parameters include:

- TMEAN = yearly (long term) mean average temperature (degrees C)
- nyears = harvest age
- nc = number of columns in the stand
- nr = number of rows in the stand
- px = spacing (feet) between columns
- py = spacing (feet) between rows
- g0MEAN = average total height of the trees in the stand at age 25
- numcln = number of clones, if any, to be used (numcln = 0 indicates a non-clonal stand established from seedlings using selected tree materials)

In addition, when clonal blocks are used:

- rspb = number of rows of trees per block
- cspb = number of columns of trees per block
- bspr = number of rows of blocks in the stand
- bspc = number of columns of blocks in the stand

In the model, each 'tree' is a pair of fundamental parameter values assigned by the user or chosen randomly from default distributions specified in the code. These parameters are:

- **g0** = 'expected' height (feet) at age 25 (roughly, an individual tree site index)
- **r0** = the constitutive resin flow rate which determines the rate resin flows from holes in the tree bark made by attacking beetles; the actual (current) flow rate, called 'resin,' changes daily as beetle penetrations and tree replenishment occur

Unless a user specifies otherwise, **r0** values follow a gamma distribution, as described in Roberds and others (2003), while **g0** values are normally distributed. In the case of clonally generated materials, specifically selected for rapid growth, **g0** values are chosen from the upper tail of a distribution having a higher mean than the distributions used for non-clonal stands, but **r0** values are randomly generated from the same gamma distribution whether or not clones are used. Regardless of how these genotypic growth and resin rates are assigned, 'site effects' are added when trees are planted. Details are in section V.B.

[**Note**: Although laboratory studies suggest that resin compounds are toxic to SPB (Coyne and Lott 1976), most field studies show little or no effective resin toxicity (Personal communication. 1999. F.P. Hain, Professor, Department of Entomology, N.C. State University, Raleigh, NC 27695-7613). Hence, in the current version of **SPBLOB** we assign a default value of 0.0 to the toxicity parameter included in the code. However, unrestricted user toxicity choices can be introduced via changes in the source code.]

C.2.1. Non-clonal Stands—Subroutine NOCLONE
If a non-clonal stand is indicated (numcln = 0), subroutine **NOCLONE** is called to set the numbers of rows and columns in the stand, after which each individual tree's (**g0,r0**) pair is randomly chosen from the distributions described.

C.2.2. Stands Using Clonal Materials—Subroutines DEPLOY and CLONE
In clonal plantings, all trees of any particular clone have the **same** pair of **g0** and **r0** values. Thus, if numcln > 0, indicating that clones are to be used, we generate only a limited number (numcln) of pairs, the default procedure being to choose randomly and independently from distributions appropriate to clonal materials. However, users may specify their own pairs as desired.

Once clones are selected the question becomes one of deployment. If clones are to be planted in blocks, each parameter pair is assigned to trees in the same number of blocks. (There are some restrictions inherent in such plantings, as indicated in chapter III.) The general patterns included in the code are:

- **RM** Randomly Mixed clonal ramets—There are clones, and the *previously chosen* parameter pairs are sampled randomly, with replacement, until parameters are assigned to all trees in the stand
- **CB** Clonal Blocks—There are clones, and trees are planted in a mosaic of clonal blocks, each block containing trees of a single clone

D. Simulating the Planted Stand

Simulation of a stand consists of four stages:

- Tree survival and growth through an 8-year juvenile period
- From age 9 until harvest, yearly updates of tree growth and mortality related to competition
- Also beginning in year 9, daily updates occur for numbers of SPB on each tree and for the tree mortality they cause (as indicated in figure 1, some particularly frequent beetle activities are updated four times per day)
- Timber harvest

D.1. The Tree Juvenile Period—Subroutine JUVEN

Because beetles are rarely of consequence in very young stands, the first 8 years are treated as a single juvenile period in which there is no beetle activity and through which tree growth and mortality are projected in one step using subroutine **JUVEN** (adapted from **PTAEDA2** with permission; see Burkhart and others 1987, Daniels and Burkhart 1975). This routine randomly assigns appropriate tree mortality during the period, then, based on the previously assigned growth rates and competition via **PTAEDA2**, computes each surviving tree's height, crown ratio, and d.b.h.

D.2. Setting Beetle Population Parameters— Subroutine PARBTL

If a simulation involves beetles, migration into and out of the stand occurs during randomly selected years from year 9 until stand harvest. In addition, there are beetle population changes related to beetle activities that occur within the stand:

- Survival
- Movement
- Oviposition
- Juvenile maturation

Rates of these SPB processes depend principally on temperature (Coulson 1980, Payne 1980, Stephen and Lih 1985, Ungerer and others 1999, Wagner and others 1984a, Wagner and others 1984b). At the beginning of stand year 9, subroutine **PARBTL** applies temperature-dependent formulas for SPB vital rates drawn from Ungerer and others (1999) and Wagner and others (1984a) to compute daily rates of oviposition and juvenile maturation for each temperature between 1 °C and 45 °C. These rates are stored in an array and used throughout the remainder of the simulation.

In addition to temperature, rates of beetle survival and movement depend on resin flows and pheromone levels associated with individual trees. These rates are recomputed daily as population updates proceed (see section E.5).

E. Age 9 Until Harvest—SIMUL and Its Subroutines

Control now passes to subroutine **SIMUL** (fig. 1). The first task is to call subroutines **OUTPUT** and **STANDINFO**, the first to compute, and the second to summarize overall stand status (number of surviving trees, total merchantable timber volume) as of the end of the 8-year juvenile period. In each stand year thereafter, we begin by assessing tree growth and mortality related to intrastand tree competition, then turn to the complex processes that take place daily within the beetle populations on each tree.

E.1. Tree Growth and Mortality Related to Intrastand Competition

At the beginning of each year from stand age 9 until harvest, total merchantable timber in the stand is computed using **PTAEDA2** subroutine **OUTPUT** (Burkhart and others 1987, Daniels and Burkhart 1975). Subroutines **COMP2** and **GROW2**, also adapted from **PTAEDA2**, then project tree growth and mortality due to competition in that year (fig. 1).

E.1.1. Merchantable Timber Volume—Subroutine OUTPUT
This subroutine computes an estimate of the total merchantable timber volume (cubic feet) of all live trees in the stand, based on each tree's height and d.b.h. (Simulation results are reported in cubic feet per acre; see, e.g., sections III.B.2.1.2 and IV.B.2) The original code (see Burkhart and others 1987, Daniels and Burkhart 1975) offers a variety of options for computing volume. In **OUTPUT**, the volume computed is total 'inside bark' volume of trees whose diameters exceed 4.5 inches (in **PTAEDA** notation, d.b.h. > 5.0). For this computation, 'volume' includes only that part of the tree bole between stump height and the upper point at which the diameter = 4 inches.

E.1.2. Tree Competition Indices—Subroutine COMP2
This subroutine computes the 'competition index' of each tree, T, as:

$$cip(T) = \Sigma \; [diam(A)/diam(T)] \; /dist(A,T)$$

where

diam(A) and diam(T) = the respective diameters (in inches) of trees
A and T
dist(A,T) = the distance (in feet) between the two trees
The sum extends over all trees A for which dist(A,T), in feet, is
numerically < 2.75*diam(A), in inches

E.1.3. Tree Growth and Mortality—Subroutine GROW2

Here, the code computes individual tree mortality and growth associated with intrastand tree competition in each year. For each particular tree, T, the *probability* that T survives tree competition during a year is given by:

$$plive = [1.028*(cr**0.038)]*exp[-0.0023*(cip(T)**2.65)]$$

where

cr = the crown ratio of tree T (vertical length of the crown as a fraction of
the total height of the tree)
cip(T) is as computed
exp denotes the exponential function

In the simulation, tree T survives the year if a uniform random deviate drawn from the interval 0.0 to 1.0 is smaller than plive.

Tree growth is computed as a function of height and diameter increments (see the **SPBLOB** source code or Burkhart and others 1987 for details). These increments are then used together with stand age to determine new values for tree height, diameter, crown ratio, crown length, and bole area.

E.2. Setting Beetle-Related Stand and Tree Parameters—Subroutine BEGYR

If the simulated stand contains beetles, at the beginning of each year subroutine **BEGYR** reinitializes each tree's maximum resin flow rate to account for tree age. Since the current (2008) literature on resin flow is inconclusive, the present version of the code sets the updated value, called RMAX, equal to the initially assigned value, r0, throughout a tree's life. However, any desired sequence of yearly changes can be introduced through changes in the source code. A few beetle-related counts are also reinitialized at this point.

E.3. Daily Simulation of Lightning Strikes—Subroutine LIGHTNING

As many as 30 to 45 percent of all SPB-caused 'spots' of tree mortality in loblolly stands originate in lightning-struck trees (Coulson and others 1983, Hodges and Pickard 1971). In the model code, simulation of each day's activity begins with random generation of a Poisson distributed number and location of lightning strikes occurring that day. The daily mean number of strikes depends on both the day of the year and the geographical location of the stand (Coulson and others 1983, fig. 1), and can be user-assigned by changing one line in the source code. Section V.E gives the details.

E.4. Daily Updates of Beetle Populations on Each Tree and of the Tree Mortality They Cause—Subroutines TEMP Through DISPERSE

As noted in the model, SPB can enter the stand as early as stand age 9. Because beetles arriving on a tree decide quickly whether to attack or move on (Bunt and others 1980), beetle populations at individual trees are updated as many as four times per day, depending on temperature.

Model recursions track only the female portion of the population, the male population in each tree being assumed equal to the number of female parents already in the tree at the beginning of a day. Repelling male pheromone levels are computed from this number, while attracting female pheromone production depends on the number of successful bark penetrations by females that day.

A model update begins with all beetles in the stand located on particular trees, those on each tree being grouped into three categories: Landed, Parent, and Juvenile. Landed beetles are on the tree exterior and engage in such activities as walking more or less aimlessly, active searching, investigation of existing entrance holes, and fighting with other SPB (Bishir and others 2004, Bunt and others 1980). Parents are adults that entered the tree previously and are engaged in gallery construction and oviposition. Juveniles are immature beetles, including eggs, larvae, and teneral adults, inside the tree bark.

Beetle mortality is assessed in every update period, while other activities, such as oviposition and juvenile maturation, occur only when simulated temperatures exceed 7 °C (Gagne and others 1982, Thatcher 1967, Ungerer and others 1999, Wagner and others 1984a).

Figure 2 shows how category populations in and on a particular tree change during an update. All beetle categories suffer natural mortality, for which no arrows are shown. In the figure, landed beetles either leave or attack. Those that do not attack enter a temporary group that will disperse from the tree at the end of the update period. Attackers either die from resin flow or predation or successfully enter the tree to become parents. Parent beetles oviposit and, when their egg production in a tree is completed, reemerge to join the dispersing group. Juveniles gain maturity and those that reach full adulthood emerge and join the group of departing beetles.

Other arrows correspond to beetles that leave or enter the stand, or those that disperse within the stand at the end of the update. For each individual tree, the new beetles that arrive, either via dispersal from other trees or by immigration from outside the stand, constitute the landed beetles with which the next update begins.

Because the timing of the attack process varies from tree to tree on any particular day, beetles at all stages of development usually exist in the stand. Thus we cannot speak meaningfully of beetle 'generations,' and must treat each day's new eggs as a separate juvenile cohort (Coulson 1980, Coulson and others 1977, Curry and others 1978, Sharpe and others 1977). Members of each cohort have their own level of maturity, determined by temperatures experienced since they entered the population. On days with sufficiently high temperatures, each cohort's maturity level increases. Those cohorts attaining full maturity emerge to join the dispersers, while new eggs are placed in a cohort of their own.

E.4.1. Generating Daily Temperatures—Subroutine TEMP

Because of the fundamental role of temperature, each simulated day begins with subroutine **TEMP**, which generates the day's high, low, and average temperatures. We assume long-term daily average temperatures follow a sine curve, with yearly average and amplitude appropriate to the geographical location of the stand. Successive daily temperatures are correlated by setting the expected average temperature for a day equal to the average of the observed mean of the previous day

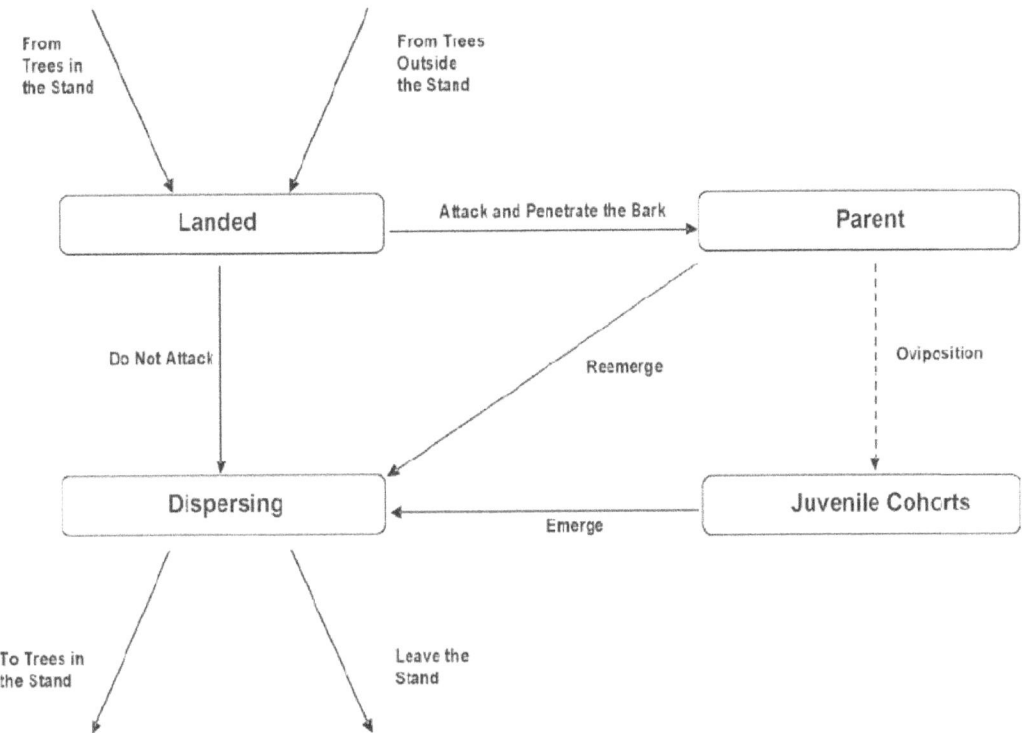

From
Trees in
the Stand

From Trees
Outside
the Stand

Landed

Attack and Penetrate the Bark

Parent

Do Not Attack

Reemerge

Oviposition

Dispersing

Emerge

Juvenile Cohorts

To Trees in
the Stand

Leave the
Stand

Figure 2—Flow of beetles among behavioral categories during daily updates in SPBLOB. Solid arrows indicate movement of individual beetles and the dashed arrow represents contribution of parents to progeny.

and the long-term average for the day's date. A day's actual high, low, and average temperatures are then randomly obtained from a normal distribution centered at this expected (mean) value. Details can be found in the source code and in Baskerville and Emin (1969). Also see section V.D.

E.4.2. Today's Oviposition Rate—Subroutine EGG

This routine computes **eggpro**, the expected proportion of her total egg complement that each surviving female parent will deposit on a particular day (Coulson and others 1978, Gagne and others 1982). This quantity is determined as a function of the day's temperatures that were generated by subroutine **TEMP**.

E.5. (Continuation of section E.4) Command Central for the Simulation Code—Subroutine UPDATE

Our model differs from others in the literature in the detail to which it simulates, on a day-by-day and tree-by-tree basis, the fundamental activities—mortality, oviposition, juvenile maturation—that govern beetle population dynamics and that cause tree damage and death during the attack process, which allows beetle reproduction to take place. Subroutine **UPDATE** represents the core of this simulation activity. It calls the subroutines **COLD, DIFFUSE, ATTACK, ENDOFDAY,** and **DISPERSE,** which compute updates of the beetle populations on each tree, and the tree damage these populations cause. (**DIFFUSE, ATTACK,** and **DISPERSE** are called four times each day, while the others are called once each day.)

E.5.1. Imposing Winter Mortality—Subroutine COLD

To begin each day, subroutine **COLD** computes beetle mortality, if any, caused by overnight low temperatures. Beetle populations can plummet during very cold temperatures, the pupal stage being most severely affected. Temperature-dependent mortality rates are modeled using normal distributions (Ungerer and others 1999). Details are in section V.F.

E.5.2. The Spread of SPB Pheromones—Subroutine DIFFUSE

Simulation experiments suggest that the compact, contiguous forms typical of observed SPB 'spots' require two phenomena:

- Rapid diffusion of pheromones through the stand (in our simulations, 'rapid' means 'by the next stand update')

- For most of the beetles departing from a tree, movement in the same direction within the stand

The second of these requirements is achieved in subroutine **DISPERSE**. Prior to that, subroutine **DIFFUSE** computes the day's positive and negative pheromone concentrations surrounding each tree. These pheromone plumes then spread throughout the stand. Based on observations obtained with an atmospheric tracer gas (Thistle and others 2004), if pheromone production at a tree T results in a concentration there of level C, this leads in the model to a concentration of 0.9C in the first ring of trees around T, a level of $(0.9)^2C$ in the second ring, and so on. The total concentration near any tree, A, is the sum (superposition) of the levels induced by beetles in all trees in the stand. Details appear in the file **spblob_params_phero_diffusion.doc** contained in the **Supporting Information** folder (see section V.A).

E.5.3. Beetle Penetration of Tree Bark—Subroutine ATTACK

Because beetles attack only living trees, all those that land by chance on dead trees during the preceding update must depart. For each living tree, landed beetles attack or leave independently, with probabilities determined by tree status. Details are in section V.H.

E.5.4. Tree Death from Beetle Penetrations

Following Hodges and others (1979) and Fargo and others (1978) we assume the number of beetle penetrations, per square meter of bole surface area, needed to kill a tree is a normal random variable, W, having mean $\mu = 64*sqrt(RMAX)$ and standard deviation $\sigma = 6.4*sqrt(RMAX)$. (RMAX is defined in section E.2). This means, for instance, that Pr(a tree having RMAX = 1.0 dies from 70 or fewer penetrations per square meter bole surface area) = $Pr(W \leq 70) = 0.8258$. Daily computations of tree mortality using code subroutine **ENDOFDAY** proceed as in the following example.

Example: Suppose that in preceding days, surviving tree T, for which the RMAX value is 1.0, has already suffered a total of 64 successful penetrations per unit bole area. If by day's end the new total is 70, then

$$Pr(T \text{ dies today}) = Pr(W \leq 70 \mid W > 64) = Pr(64 < W \leq 70)/Pr(W > 64)$$
$$= (0.8258 - 0.5)/0.5 = 0.6516$$

Section V.I contains a more general discussion.

E.5.5. Summing up the Day's Activities—Subroutine ENDOFDAY

For each tree, this subroutine computes:

- The total number of eggs laid during the observed day—based on the proportion **eggpro**, computed in subroutine **EGG**

- The number of parents that reemerge—based on Coulson and others (1978) and Gagne and others (1982), the *proportion* of parents that reemerge is assumed equal to **eggpro**

- The number of remaining parents that survive

- The new productions of attracting and repelling pheromones proportional, respectively, to the number of successful tree penetrations by female SPB during the day, and to the number of males in the tree

- The day's quantity of resin flow from the tree—dependent on tree resin level and the number of beetle attacks that day

- The new maturity levels attained by beetles in each juvenile cohort

- The cumulative number of newly mature brood adults that emerged during the day's four updates

Based on these computations, each tree's list of juvenile cohorts is updated by inserting the new eggs and removing those juveniles that emerged upon reaching maturity. (These newly emerged brood adults are added to the group of departing adults, as described.) Finally, the trees that succumb to beetle attack are identified and killed. See sections V.I.2 and V.J for details.

E.5.6. Moving the Departing Adult Beetles—Subroutine DISPERSE

As suggested in section E.5.2, development of cohesive infestations depends on movement of most departing beetles toward roughly the same stand location. This is accomplished in **DISPERSE** by moving all beetles departing from each particular tree T to the tree situated at most one row or column removed from T that currently has the highest positive (attracting) pheromone level. Details are in section V.L.

Coda: This completes the general description of the **SPBLOB** source code structure and the tasks performed by individual code subroutines. For user convenience, this source code has been used to generate both an executable interactive code for single stand simulations in which users have wide latitude in choosing values of stand attributes—such as number of rows and columns (spacing), and time of harvest—and an executable version that simulates multiple, independent replications of a more limited list of stand scenarios. These two executable codes differ considerably in input data requirements and in output produced, and for this reason are discussed separately. Users interested in the **Interactive** version should consult chapter III, while those wishing **Multiple** replicates are referred to chapter IV.

III. USER GUIDE TO IMPLEMENTATION OF THE INTERACTIVE WINDOWS-BASED SPBLOB CODE

A. Introduction—Downloading and Installing SPBLOB on Your Machine

SPBLOB is a software package that simulates the joint population dynamics of southern pine beetle and loblolly pine, from time of stand planting until harvest. An **executable interactive version** of the **SPBLOB** code is available at **www.srs.fs.usda.gov/idip/** as part of the overall package of materials that constitute **SPBLOB**. To obtain these materials:

- Go to the Web site
- Click on the button **'SPB & Invasive Insects'**
- Look under the heading **'RESEARCH TOOLS'**
- Click on the category **'Simulation Models'**
- On the **'Simulation Models'** page click on the button **'SPBLOB'**
- On the **'WELCOME TO SPBLOB'** page read the **Introduction** section, then follow instructions for downloading and using **SPBLOB**

The rest of chapter III concerns the **Interactive** version of the code. Chapter II contains background information concerning the code structure, while chapter IV discusses use of the **Multiple-Simulation** version of the code. For those users who want to tailor the source code to their own specifications, we include detailed information in chapter V and in the **Supporting Information** files in **SPBLOB_Folder_9-29-08**. All **SPBLOB** codes and supporting files are contained in the **SPBLOB** folder you downloaded.

B. Running the Interactive Version of SPBLOB

In addition to the file **tree.exe**, the **interactive** folder in **spblob_11_27_2007** contains a file called **input.txt**. This file consists of a list of 7000 randomly generated pairs of seeds useful for running code simulations and provides the potential for a large number of independent simulations. When, as instructed, you open **tree.exe**, the program randomly chooses one of these seed pairs with which to begin the simulation. (The line chosen will be indicated in the output file generated after simulation is complete; see section B.2). Successive simulations thus produce a variety of results, and you may want to simulate several stands to get a feel for the possibilities.

Note: In order for the **Interactive** code to run properly, its **tree.exe** and **input** files must remain together in the **interactive** folder. Do not separate these files or remove them from the folder.

Roughly speaking, an interactive session using **SPBLOB** consists of two major phases:

- An **Input Phase**, in which you specify the particular features you want your simulated stand to possess

- An **Output Phase**, in which you receive yearly information about the status of the stand as the simulation proceeds, and a detailed overall summary at the end. Some of this information appears on the screen as the simulation proceeds, but a more extensive summary appears in two output files produced at the end.

B.1. The Interactive, Input Phase of SPBLOB

The first thing you see upon opening **tree.exe** is this window:

```
[cn] C:\tree\interactive\tree.exe                                                          _ [ ] X
     ---------------------------------------------------------------------------------
     |        Loblolly Pine Tree Growth Simulation with Beetle Dynamics       |
     |                                                                        |
     |   By: John Bishir, Xiaohai Wan,        James Roberds, Brian Strom      |
     |        Mathematics Department              USDA Forest Service         |
     |     North Carolina State University    Southern Research Station       |
     |          Raleigh, NC 27695                        USA                  |
     ---------------------------------------------------------------------------------
     User can interrupt the simulation at any time by closing the window.

     Do you wish to continue? <Yes or No>: _
```

If you answer "no" or "n", the session terminates.

If you answer "yes" or "y", you are presented with a series of on-screen requests that allow you to specify attributes of the stand you wish to simulate. These are discussed in section B.1.

If you enter any other response, the simulation will not proceed, but will pause and wait for "yes" or "no".

Let us assume you answer "yes" to the question on the screen. In order to set up the simulation with the type of stand you want, you will now be presented a series of questions/requests that appear on your monitor. In each case, type your preferred response and press **Return**.

Note: You can terminate the session at any time by closing the window.

Temperature is the most important determinant of SPB vital rates (movement, mortality, oviposition, survival). For this reason, **SPBLOB** first asks you to specify the mean annual temperature at your stand location. (Examples—the mean annual temperatures in Houston, TX, Jackson, MS and Raleigh, NC are about 19 °C, 17 °C and 15 °C, respectively. But any value you choose—positive, negative, or zero—is accommodated.) Here is what you see on the screen:

```
Yearly mean temperature (Celsius) at stand location: e.g., 15.00
    Input your value:
```

Next, there are questions about stand duration and geometry.

```
Number of growing seasons: e.g., 35
    Input your value (must be at least 9 years):
```

Note: The number of growing seasons specified can be as large as 1,000, so any realistic value is accommodated. Simulation time is roughly proportional to the number of years simulated, and to the number of trees in the stand. Depending on the particular machine used, our simulations of 35-year stands having 32 rows and columns require from 3 to 7 minutes, on average, so, for example, most 100-year stands of that size would run 9 to 21 minutes, while a 100 x 100 stand, on average, will require 12 to 40 minutes to run to a harvest age of 35 years.

Note: Some of the remaining questions require "yes" or "no" responses, but most ask for numerical input. There are **no restrictions** on these numbers **except** that they must be positive (not zero or negative).

```
Spacing between rows (feet): e.g., 9.84
    Input your value:
```

```
Spacing between columns (feet): e.g., 9.84
    Input your value:
```

As indicated in chapter II, in **SPBLOB** each 'tree' is a pair of parameter values:

- **g0** = tree growth rate, the 'site index' associated with that tree (see section II.C.2)
- **r0** = the constitutive resin flow rate which governs the rate at which resin flows from holes in the tree bark produced by beetles

The code always generates resin flow rates using the 'ordinary' gamma(α,β) distribution described in Roberds and others (2003). On the other hand, growth rates are randomly and independently generated using a normal distribution for which you are asked to specify the mean μ. (This mean represents a 'site index'—see **Note** on top of page 18. By default, the standard deviation of the distribution is $\sigma = 5$ feet.)

Thus, the next question is:

```
Stand site index (feet): e.g., 80.0000
    Input your value:
```

Note: This 'site index' of the tree represents the expected (average) height, in feet, a tree will attain by age 25.

In **SPBLOB**, there are three principal stand types available:

- 'Ordinary' stands, planted with improved tree materials derived from any source, e.g., improved stock from a seed orchard
- Stands planted using 'clonally generated' materials, the clonal ramets that make up the stand being randomly mixed before planting
- Stands planted using clonally generated materials, the clonal ramet being planted in blocks, all ramets in any particular block belonging to the same clone

Thus, the next question is:

```
Will the stand be planted using clonal materials? (Yes or No):
```

If you answer "no" or "n", the screen skips to the questions in the subsection headed 'B.1.5 No Clones', near the end of this section B, and you can now move directly to that point in this guide.

If you answer "yes" or "y" (clonal materials should be used), you will be asked to respond to a series of questions about these clones. The first is:

```
Will clone ramets be planted in clonal blocks? (Yes or No):
```

If you answer "no" or "n", the screen skips to the section headed 'B.1.1. Number of Clones When Blocks Are Not Used.' Please move to that point on page 19 in this guide and continue from there.

If you answer "yes" or "y", there are requests for information concerning these blocks.

Note: In any simulation involving clonal blocks, the stand is created by specifying the size and arrangement of the individual blocks. All blocks in any particular simulation are the same size; however, this size can vary from one simulation to another. The information requests are:

```
Single block size
    Number of rows: e.g., 16
    Input your value:

    Number of columns: e.g., 16
    Input your value:
```

```
Number of blocks
    In row direction: e.g., 2
    Input your value:

    In column direction: e.g., 2
    Input your value:
```

Then, you see a message on the screen indicating the effect on stand size of your choices so far:

```
***  Your stand size is: x  by  y,
```

where

x = (# rows per block)*(# blocks in the row direction)
y = (# columns per block)*(# blocks in the column direction)

You can now skip to the section 'B.1.2 More Information Related to Blocks' on page 20.

B.1.1. Number of Clones When Blocks Are Not Used

At this juncture we need to specify the number of clones and the parameters that define these clones. Acceptable values of these quantities depend on stand size and on whether blocks are to be used. If there are no clonal blocks, you see these requests on the screen:

```
Stand size:
    Number of rows: e.g., 32
    Input your value:

    Number of columns: e.g., 32
    Input your value:

How many clones do you want to use? (must be a factor of
[# rows]*[# columns])
    Input your value:
```

Note: The restriction is of no real consequence. For example, if your stand contained 32 rows and 32 columns, the requirement would read "must be a factor of 1024," allowing numbers far in excess of the practical limit of 30 to 40 clones (see, e.g., Bishir and Roberds 1995, 1997, 1999; Libby 1982; Roberds and Bishir 1997; Roberds and others 1990). It appears only because in **SPBLOB** we want to plant the same number of ramets of each clone used. This requires the number of clones to be a divisor of the total number of trees in the stand.

If you are not using clonal blocks, you can skip to section 'B.1.3 Parameter Values' on page 20.

B.1.2. More Information Related to Blocks

When your stand is formed using blocks of clones, you see:

```
How many clones do you want to use?  (must be a factor of w)
   Input your value:
```

Note: The number w that appears on your screen is equal to

w = total # of blocks

= (# blocks in the row direction)*(# blocks in the column direction)

because in **SPBLOB**, if clones are planted in blocks, each clone is used in the same number of blocks.

B.1.3. Clonal Parameter Values

Now some questions about clonal parameter values:

```
Do you want to specify the growth and resin flow parameters
for each clone?
   (Yes or No):
```

If you answer "no" or "n", you see

```
*** The growth and resin flow rates for the clones are:
```

followed by a list of randomly generated values for your stand.

Note: To reflect the fact that clones are typically chosen due to their elevated growth rates, the random values of **g0** are generated by censoring the normal distribution whose mean you specified so that only the top 15 percent—those with growth rates exceeding $\mu + 1.065\sigma$—are accepted.

User assigned parameter values, on the other hand, are unrestricted. Thus,

If you answer "yes" or "y", indicating that you prefer to set your own growth and resin flow rates (denoted by **g0** and **r0**, respectively; see section V.B.2 for units), you see (repeated for each integer x from 1 up to n = number of clones):

```
Enter your desired parameters for clone # x:
   Input a value for g0:
   Input a value for r0:
```

Finally, whether **SPBLOB** generated the clone parameters, or you did, clonal ramets must be deployed in the stand.

If your clones are **not** planted in blocks, there is one more question.

```
Should the clones be deployed randomly in the stand? (Yes or No):
```

If you answer "yes" or "y", **SPBLOB** will randomly mix clonal ramets
throughout the stand, taking care to plant about the same number
of ramets of each clone. The pattern of assignment of clone numbers will
then appear on the screen, followed by the beginning of simulation output.
Details are in section B.2.

If, however, you answer "no" or "n", **SPBLOB** will ask you to assign a clone
number to every tree, one at a time. Since this can be quite time-consuming
(e.g., a 32 x 32 stand will require 1,024 choices), this choice should be avoided
unless there are strong reasons for pursuing it.

In either case, you can skip in this guide to the heading 'B.1.4 Wrapup When Clones
Are Being Used' on page 22.

If, however, your clones are to be deployed in blocks, there is one
additional query:

```
Should the clones be assigned randomly to blocks? (Yes or No):
```

If you answer "yes" or "y", the pattern of this placement will appear on the
screen, where you will see:

```
*** The arrangement of clonal blocks in your stand is:
```

followed by an array of numbers indicating the stand positions in which
SPBLOB has randomly placed the clones (each clone will appear in the
same number of blocks).

If you answer "no" or "n", you can assign clones to blocks in whatever pattern
and in whatever frequencies you wish. For each block (x,y), you will be asked
for the:

```
Clone number for block x,y:
Input a value:
```

where

x runs from 1 to nrsb = number of rows of blocks
y runs from 1 to ncsb = number of columns of blocks

Note: The clone numbers you assign cannot exceed the number of clones you
specified earlier.

Note: Now that growth and resin flow rates have been specified for each clone, **SPBLOB** will plant the individual trees in the stand according to the instructions you have given. Whether ramets are randomly distributed in the stand or are planted in clonal blocks, each ramet of a particular clone type is assigned the *same* pair of growth and resin flow values as the other ramets within its clone (these values differ from one clone to another). However, some variation is achieved between ramets of the same clone by adding randomly and independently distributed deviations to each tree's growth and resin flow values, thus modeling heterogeneous environmental factors (site variation) at different stand locations.

B.1.4. Wrapup When Clones Are Being Used

This ends the input required when clones are used. Whether **SPBLOB** assigned clones to blocks, or you did, simulation now begins immediately, and you see these two lines on the screen:

```
Stand setup is complete, simulation in progress

Clone # = 0 indicates the whole stand
```

followed by a report on stand status at the end of the juvenile stage (end of year 8). Following this, there will be pauses between the subsequent yearly reports as computation proceeds.

A detailed discussion of simulation output appears in section B.2. Here, we note only that output lines labeled 'clone # = 0' contain reports for the whole stand, while lines designated 'clone # = n', where n is a positive integer, report output for clone # n alone.

B.1.5. No Clones

When a stand is planted using improved materials, but not clones, we need only to specify the size of the stand:

```
Overall stand size:

    Number of rows: e.g., 32
    Input your value:

    Number of columns: e.g., 32
    Input your value:
```

B.2. Simulation Output

SPBLOB will now plant the stand you have specified, assigning randomly and independently chosen growth and resin flow values, as well as adding randomly and independently distributed deviations to the tree growth and resin flow values. As a result heterogeneous environmental factors (site effects) are modeled throughout the stand. On the screen, you will see:

```
Stand setup is complete, simulation in progress

Clone # = 0 indicates the whole stand
```

followed by a report on stand status as of the end of the juvenile stage (end of year 8).

Note: Clone # = 0 is used to indicate the entire stand, whether or not clones are actually used in stand setup.

The first line on the screen precedes the data from year 8 and looks like:

```
Stand Age     Clone #      Merch.Vol.   Percent Surv.Trees     Immi
```

This line will be followed by yearly reports on the screen about the status of the stand as the simulation proceeds. In these reports,

- **Stand Age** is expressed in **years** since stand planting

- **Clone #** = 0 corresponds to the entire stand; if clones are used, remaining lines run from 1 to numcln (the total number of clones used in this simulation)

- **Merch. Vol**. is the total merchantable timber volume (cubic feet per acre) currently available in the stand (**Clone #** = 0) or from trees in each clone (**Clone #** = 1 to numcln)

- **Percent Surv. Trees** is the percentage of that clone's planted trees that still survive

- **Immi** = 'false' appears in the first line (**Clone #** = 0) if there was no beetle immigration that year; if beetles did arrive, then **Immi** = 'true' appears in that line. The value of **Immi** does not appear in the lines corresponding to individual clones

Notes:

- These five items along with several others, are written to an output file (see section B.2.1).

- On a PC, a 32 x 32 stand will require 1 to 10 minutes of CPU time to run. Average run time is roughly proportional to the total number of trees in the stand. (On our own machines the average run time is about 3 minutes.) Time differences between simulations of same-size stands are due primarily to random variations in the number of stand years during which beetles migrate into the stand.

- In principle, there is no limit on stand size. However, practical limitations on the amount of output storage space and on the time required for simulation argue against very large stands.

- **A caveat**—We consider the model and its accompanying simulation code primarily as investigative tools, rather than accurate predictors of stand timber volume or degree of beetle activity in particular stand scenarios. The reason is that primary beetle activities—egg production, development in juvenile stages, movement, and mortality—are largely controlled by temperature (Coulson 1980, Payne 1980, Stephen and Lih 1985, Ungerer and others 1999, Wagner and others 1984a, Wagner and others 1984b) which, in turn, is subject to unpredictable chance fluctuations. In addition, field observations indicate that in some stands beetles can appear in considerable numbers (e.g., via migration from outside) by age 10 or before, while others remain free of beetle infestations throughout their existence. Thus, model comparisons of management strategies (e.g., clonal plantings vs. stands generated from seedlings or, in clonally generated stands, block plantings vs. random mix of ramets) should be based, not on single stand simulations, but rather on averages obtained from multiple, independent replicates (discussed in chapter IV) of any proposed strategy. Comparison of individual replicates can, however, provide information about the variation in stand output to be expected among plantings. And single stand simulations by themselves can yield useful insights into beetle activities and their consequences as a stand ages.

B.2.1. What Output Information Is Saved to Files

For each stand simulation, the code saves output information in two files that are automatically created and placed in the folder 'interactive.' The first of these, identified by "t", and followed by the simulation number (line # from input.txt), stores information about each individual tree in the simulated stand. The second output file, labeled "s", and followed by the simulation #, contains yearly summaries about the stand. These outputs include all the information that appears on your screen plus several additional entries. Here are the details:

B.2.1.1. The Tree-Information Output File

Each row in a "t-file" contains 10 entries that correspond to a particular tree in the simulation. These entries appear in the sequence:

$$[\text{seed pair, i, j, r0(i,j), g0(i,j), clntyp(i,j), yrdied(i,j), daydied(i,j)}$$
$$\text{lightning(i,j), vmerch(i,j)}]$$

where

seed pair = line number used from the file input.txt
i = tree's row number in the simulated stand
j = column number of the tree
$r0(i,j)$ = constitutive resin flow rate (including site effect) for tree(i,j)
$g0(i,j)$ = growth rate (including site effect) for tree(i,j)
$clntyp(i,j)$ = number of the clone to which tree(i,j) belongs
(= 0 if clones are not used in this simulation)
$yrdied(i,j)$ = stand age (years) at which tree(i,j) died (= 0 if tree is still alive at harvest)
$daydied(i,j)$ = day of year (1 = Jan 1; 365 = Dec 31) on which tree(i,j) died
(= 0 if tree died from competition or is still alive at harvest)
$lightning(i,j)$ = cause of death of tree(i,j) (see notes below)
$vmerch(i,j)$ = merchantable volume (cubic feet) of tree(i,j) (= 0 if the tree is dead)

Notes Related to the Tree-Information File:

- In each "t-file" there is a line for each tree, each with 10 entries (1,024 lines for a 32 x 32 stand).

- Values of **r0, g0** and **clntyp** are assigned at the beginning of the simulation and constitute part of the stand initialization. On the other hand, entries in **yrdied, daydied,** and **lightning** are determined as the simulation computations proceed and are not known for all trees until the simulation ends.

- Values of **yrdied, daydied, and lightning** contain more information than is at first apparent. For instance, **yrdied(i,j)** = 0 if tree(i,j) is still alive at time of harvest, **yrdied(i,j)** = 8 indicates a tree that died during the 8-year tree juvenile period during which no beetles were present in the stand, and **yrdied(i,j)** = k > 8 means that tree(i,j) died during stand year k.

- Moreover, **daydied(i,j)** > 0 if tree(i,j) was killed by beetle penetrations **and/or** by lightning. For example, (**yrdied(i,j)** = 21, **daydied(i,j)** = 154, **lightning(i,j)** = 16) will be counted as meaning tree(i,j) was killed by beetles **and** by lightning—on day 154 (June 3) of stand year 21, 16 days after being struck. On the other hand, (**yrdied(i,j)** = 21, **daydied(i,j)** = 154, **lightning(i,j)** = 30) means the tree was killed by lightning but not by beetles, while (**yrdied(i,j)** = 21, **daydied(i,j)** = 0) means that tree(i,j) died from tree competition at the beginning of year 21, prior to that year's daily updates, and was not killed by beetles.

- To clarify further the information supplied by the **lightning** matrix, **lightning(i,j)** = 0 if tree(i,j) was never struck by lightning during the entire course of the simulation; **lightning(i,j)** = n, where 0 < n < 30, if tree(i,j) WAS struck by lightning, then died n days later as a consequence of beetle attacks; and **lightning(i,j)** = 30 means the tree was struck by lightning, not killed by beetles during the following 30 days, and died (by default, in the code) due to the original lightning strike.

- In short, from values of **yrdied, daydied,** and **lightning** we can determine *when* (year and day) and *why* (competition, lightning, beetles) each tree died, if at all. Here is the list of possibilities:

If tree(i,j) dies, then **yrdied(i,j)** > 0; in this case,
    - **daydied(i,j)** = 0 means tree(i,j) was killed by competition
    - **daydied(i,j)** > 0, **lightning(i,j)** = 0 means killed by beetles, not lightning
    - **daydied(i,j)** > 0, **lightning(i,j)** = n (0 < n < 30) means killed by beetles **and** lightning
    - **daydied(i,j)** > 0, **lightning(i,j)** = 30 means killed by lightning, not beetles

B.2.1.2. The Stand-Information Output File

In an "s-file," each row contains 18 entries that correspond to a particular clone in a particular year, within a particular simulation. These entries are arranged in the sequence:

> **[seed pair, age, immi, clone #, %treesurv, %treekill_B, %treekill_L, %treekill_C, avdiam_surv, avdiam_KB, avdiam_KC, avhgt_surv, avhgt_KB, avhgt_KC, avres_surv, avres_KB, merchvol, basal_area]**

where **seed pair** is as above, and

age = stand age in years

immi = 1 if there is beetle immigration this year, and = 0 if no immigration

clone # = identification number of the 'clone' about which info is reported (0 = entire stand)

%treesurv = for each clone, the percentage of planted trees that still survive

%treekill_B = for each clone, the percentage of planted trees killed by beetles *this* year

%treekill_L = for each clone, the percentage of planted trees killed by lightning *this* year

%treekill_C = for each clone, the percentage of planted trees killed by competition *this* year

avdiam_surv = for each clone, the average diameter (inches) for surviving trees

avdiam_KB = for each clone, the average diameter (inches) for trees killed by beetles *this* year (**)

avdiam_KC = for each clone, the average diameter (inches) for trees killed by competition *this* year (**)

avhgt_surv = for each clone, the average height (feet) for surviving trees

avhgt_KB = for each clone, the average height (feet) for trees killed by beetles *this* year (**)

avhgt_KC = for each clone, the average height (feet) for trees killed by competition *this* year (**)

avres_surv = for each clone, the average resin flow (g/24h from a 0.5-inch diameter wound) for surviving trees

avres_KB = for each clone, the average resin flow (g/24h) in trees killed by beetles up to now

merchvol = for each clone, the total merchantable timber volume (cubic feet per acre) in its surviving trees

basal_area = for each clone, the basal area (square feet per acre) in its surviving trees

Notes Related to Stand-Information Files:

- Within each "s-file," a summary line for each clone is produced at the end of each year, starting at stand age 8. (In order for the percentages to include all planted trees, the age-8 report includes all deaths that occur during the stand juvenile period.) With an average of 15 lines (1 + # of clones) per year and 28 years of output (if harvest age = 35), an average "s-file" contains approximately 15 x 28 = 420 lines, each with 18 entries.

- In the code, although competition deaths, tree diameters and tree heights are computed at the *beginning* of each year, all information recorded in "s-files" is current as of the *end* of each year, in order to also take account of the year's tree mortality due to beetles.

- The four percentages listed above can total more than 100. The reason is that trees can be killed by both beetles and by lightning (in the code, this occurs when a lightning struck tree is subsequently killed by beetles before the default 30-day period ends—see the fourth note related to the "t-files").

- Items marked by (**) differ from other closely related items in that they report on the current year, rather than being cumulative from the time of stand planting. This is because heights and diameters of killed trees can be meaningfully compared to those of surviving trees only within the year of death.

- The merchantable volume in the stand is the sum of volumes of all *surviving* trees, computed on a per acre basis. For an individual clone, the same computation is made, though here the divisor used is the area occupied only by the originally planted ramets of *that* clone, not the area of the entire stand.

- The basal area in the stand is the sum of all the cross-sectional areas of the surviving trees, computed on a per acre basis. For an individual clone, the same computation is made, though here the divisor used is the area occupied only by the originally planted ramets of *that* clone, not the area of the entire stand.

- **Warning**: When clonal ramets are randomly mixed before planting, relative magnitudes of the per-acre volumes or basal areas reported may, due to chance proximity of clones with different growth rates, not reflect true comparisons of volumes these clones would produce if planted in individual blocks.

IV. GUIDE TO USING THE MULTIPLE-SIMULATION VERSION OF SPBLOB

A. How to Run Batch Simulation Jobs

Four files are required to run the version of **SPBLOB** designed for batch simulation jobs. These files, contained in a folder called **multiple**, are:

configs.txt	**input.txt**
run.txt	**tree.exe**

Notes:

The **multiple** folder is part of the overall package of materials included in the **SPBLOB** zip file downloadable from **www.srs.fs.usda.gov/idip/**. If you do not already have these materials, you can obtain them by following the directions in the introduction to chapter III.

In order for the **Multiple** code to run properly, its four files *must* remain together in the **multiple** folder. Do not separate these files or remove them from the folder.

Though it has the same name, the **tree.exe** file indicated here is *not* the same as the one contained in the **interactive** folder discussed in chapter III.

An electronic copy of the **SPBLOB** source code is also included in the download package. (This source code is the same as that used to generate the executable **Interactive** code discussed in chapter III.) If you wish to modify the source code, e.g., to study effects of changing certain parameter values, open the relevant subroutine files and make the desired changes by editing them as you would any text file. After making your changes, set the variable "**batch**" in the subroutine **MAIN** to "1" to rebuild the **Multiple-Simulation** version (set "**batch**" to "0" to rebuild the **Interactive** version). Then compile the resulting new **Source Code**. See chapter V and appendix A for full details.

In section A.4 we indicate how to run batch simulations using the **Multiple** code. First, though, we provide a brief description of its three auxiliary files.

A.1. The File configs.txt

Each of the 23 rows of the file **configs.txt**, shown here as table 1, contains 13 entries. The first entry is the number of the **configuration** described in that row, while the second is a code related to the overall pattern in which trees are to be planted. In this code, the 1 or 2 digits (0, 1, 2, 6, 12, 18, 30, or 50) *preceding* the last digit represent the number of clones, if any, that are used in planting the stand (0 = no clones). If the number of clones is 0 or 1, the last digit identifies the mean yearly temperature (third column of the table) at the stand location. Otherwise, the *last digit* indicates the pattern in which clonal materials are to be deployed:

1 = all trees are randomly mixed before planting
2 = for each clone, all trees are planted in a single block
3 or 4 = trees of each clone are planted in more than one block
  (see parameter bspc in the list)

Table 1—The list of preprogrammed configurations developed for SPBLOB simulations

config	pattern	avtemp	nr	nc	numcln	rspb	cspb	nrsb	ncsb	bspc	dcol	drow
1	01	15	32	32	0	0	0	0	0	0	9.84	9.84
2	02	17	32	32	0	0	0	0	0	0	9.84	9.84
3	03	19	32	32	0	0	0	0	0	0	9.84	9.84
4	11	15	32	32	1	32	32	1	1	1	9.84	9.84
5	12	17	32	32	1	32	32	1	1	1	9.84	9.84
6	13	19	32	32	1	32	32	1	1	1	9.84	9.84
7	21	17	32	32	2	1	1	32	32	512	9.84	9.84
8	22	17	32	32	2	32	16	1	2	1	9.84	9.84
9	23	17	32	32	2	16	16	2	2	2	9.84	9.84
10	61	17	36	30	6	1	1	36	30	180	9.84	9.84
11	62	17	36	30	6	12	15	3	2	1	9.84	9.84
12	63	17	36	30	6	9	10	4	3	2	9.84	9.84
13	64	17	36	30	6	6	5	6	6	6	9.84	9.84
14	121	17	36	30	12	1	1	36	30	90	9.84	9.84
15	122	17	36	30	12	9	10	4	3	1	9.84	9.84
16	123	17	36	30	12	6	5	6	6	3	9.84	9.84
17	181	17	36	30	18	1	1	36	30	60	9.84	9.84
18	182	17	36	30	18	6	10	6	3	1	9.84	9.84
19	183	17	36	30	18	4	5	9	6	3	9.84	9.84
20	301	17	36	30	30	1	1	36	30	36	9.84	9.84
21	302	17	36	30	30	6	6	6	5	1	9.84	9.84
22	501	17	40	30	50	1	1	40	30	24	9.84	9.84
23	502	17	40	30	50	4	6	10	5	1	9.84	9.84

The last eleven entries in a row are parameter values for the particular **stand configuration** specified in that row. These eleven **input parameters** are:

avtemp = average annual temperature (°C) at the stand location
nr = total number of rows in the stand
nc = total number of columns in the stand
numcln = number of clones used in planting the stand (0 = no clones)
rspb = number of rows of trees in each clonal block
cspb = number of columns of trees in each clonal block
nrsb = number of rows of blocks, if any, in the stand
ncsb = number of columns of blocks, if any, in the stand
bspc = for each clone, the number of blocks, if any, in which it is planted
dcol = distance (feet) between columns in the stand
drow = distance (feet) between rows in the stand

Notes:

- The entries in table 1 can be altered to allow simulation of stands with overall sizes and internal geometries of particular interest to you. For instance, if you want to run simulations of stand configuration # 2, but for a larger stand with 60 rows and 50 columns, simply replace nr = 32 and nc = 32 with nr = 60 and nc = 50. Then re-save the file **configs.txt** and run the simulations in the usual way, as described in section A.4. (There is no need to recompile the source code, as these values are automatically read from **configs.txt** at the beginning of a simulation.)

- In simulating these configurations, clonal and/or individual tree values of **g0** and **r0** are generated randomly (see the discussions in sections II.C.2 and V.B)

- numcln = 0 indicates that no clones are used

- numcln > 0 implies use of clones in planting the stand

- If clonal blocks are used, all blocks in a particular simulation have the same size and shape, and each clone is planted in the same number of blocks

Warning: There are restrictions on the changes allowed in **configs.txt**. For instance, if you want a stand with 7 rows of clonal blocks, and 6 columns of blocks, each block containing 5 rows and 6 columns of trees, then your stand size must be 7x5 = 35 rows by 6x6 = 36 columns. Further, the total number of blocks in the stand is 7x6 = 42, which requires the number of clones to be a divisor of 42 (one of the numbers 2, 3, 6, 7, 14, 21, or 42) in order for each clone to appear in the same number of blocks. If any of these restrictions are violated, the code gives an error message, and simulation will not proceed.

A.2. The File input.txt

File **input.txt** contains a list of 7,000 randomly and independently generated pairs of integers, the first 15 of which are exhibited in table 2. As described, batch simulations are constructed by choosing groups of rows from this table. Each particular row pair leads to a different simulation, the two seeds serving to initialize random number streams that are used in all random number subroutines.

Table 2—The first 15 rows in the file input.txt

pair	first seed	second seed
1	769507989	391973004
2	786410668	766832987
3	557965049	908347825
4	143157914	657742113
5	921209698	883037717
6	24862566	688162812
7	584741353	715680511
8	785792706	505503855
9	980069746	105311691
10	520294406	844090295
11	189630999	754658824
12	519544887	172030176
13	99964747	909842805
14	985824992	19186678
15	272832311	687032720

A.3. The File run.txt

When generating multiple, independent replicates of a particular stand configuration, it is convenient to enter a single command rather than having to specify each simulation separately. The file **run.txt**, shown here as table 3, facilitates this approach. In this table, each configuration is allotted 200 simulations.

The lines from **input.txt** actually used in simulating a configuration can be changed by editing entries in table 3. For example, if you wish to run a set of 50 independent replicates of configuration #15, beginning with line (seed pair) #3842, and with harvest age = 40 years, simply change the row entries to read:

15   122   3842   3891   40

Then re-save the file.

Table 3—The file run.txt. Beginning with the third row of the table (config # 1), row entries under the headings "First Line" and "Last Line" designate the line numbers in the file input.txt that are reserved for simulation of the stand configuration indicated in the row

config	pattern	Lines Reserved in input.txt		Harvest Age
		First Line	Last Line	
1	01	1001	1200	35
2	02	1201	1400	35
3	03	1401	1600	35
4	11	1601	1800	35
5	12	1801	2000	35
6	13	2001	2200	35
7	21	2201	2400	35
8	22	2401	2600	35
9	23	2601	2800	35
10	61	2801	3000	35
11	62	3001	3200	35
12	63	3201	3400	35
13	64	3401	3600	35
14	121	3601	3800	35
15	122	3801	4000	35
16	123	4001	4200	35
17	181	4201	4400	35
18	182	4401	4600	35
19	183	4601	4800	35
20	301	4801	5000	35
21	302	5001	5200	35
22	501	5201	5400	35
23	502	5401	5600	35

A.4. The File tree.exe

This is the executable code file that does the work of running repeated, independent stand simulations that you have specified, as described in the paragraph above. This executable code also writes simulation results to output files, the contents of which are discussed in section B. Here, we describe how to run a batch of simulations.

As noted in section A, four files are required to run the version of **SPBLOB** designed for batch simulation jobs. These files, contained in the folder called **multiple,** are:

configs.txt	**input.txt**
run.txt	**tree.exe**

Warning: Though it has the same name, the **tree.exe** file indicated here is *not* the same as the one contained in the **interactive** folder discussed in chapter III. To avoid confusion, and to obtain proper results, all code files must remain in their respective folders. In addition, the procedure described for running multiple simulations differs in several respects from that used for the interactive simulations discussed in chapter III (that procedure will not work here).

As indicated in section A.2, seed pairs from the file **input.txt** are dedicated (as specified in the file **run.txt**; see section A.3) to each of the 23 stand scenarios listed in table 1. With this arrangement, a single command suffices to run all the replicates associated with a particular configuration of interest (see the second the paragraph in section A.3).

For example, suppose you want to run independent replicates of stand scenario # 15. The first step is to move to the directory **multiple** that contains the four code files necessary for batch simulation. If, as instructed in section III.A, these files are saved in "C" drive (C directory),

• Click "Run" in the "Start" menu

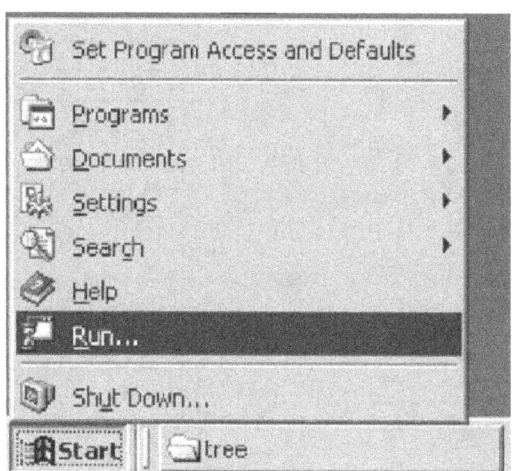

- In the "Run" window, type **cmd** to open the "Command" window, and then click "OK" to finish

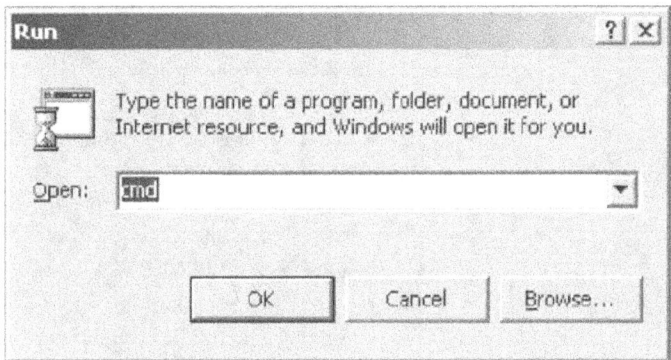

- In the Command Window, type **C:** and press the enter key to access the C drive
- On the screen you will see **C:\>**. Now type **cd spblob_11_27_2007\multiple** (updated versions of the codes and folders will have later dates) to enter the folder called **multiple**
- Finally, type **tree 15** (the word "tree" followed by a space and the number of the configuration you want to simulate) and press enter

This last action starts the simulations. On the screen, a heading and one or more rows of output data will follow immediately. The heading looks like this:

```
Stand Age     Clone #      Merch.Vol.    Percent Surv. Trees      Immi
```

The output rows that follow appear in groups, each group corresponding to 1 year of stand simulation. The first group you will see represents a summary of the stand status at the end of the 8-year juvenile tree stage.

A glance at table 1 shows that stand configuration # 15 involves 12 clones, planted in separate blocks containing 9 rows and 10 columns each. In this case, each yearly group of output consists of 13 rows, the first having 5 entries, the others 4 entries each. In these rows:

- **Stand Age** is expressed in years since stand planting
- **Clone #** = 0 corresponds to the entire stand; remaining values indicate clones 1 through 12
- **Merch. Vol.** is the total merchantable timber volume (cubic feet per acre) currently available in the stand (clone # = 0) or from surviving trees in individual clones (1-12)
- **Percent Surv. Trees** is the percentage of a clone's originally planted trees that still survive
- **Immi** = "false" appears in the first line (clone # = 0) if there was no beetle immigration that year; if beetles did arrive, then **Immi** = "true" in that line. The value of **Immi** is not repeated in the lines corresponding to individual clones

Notes:

- On a PC, a 32 x 32 stand will require 1 to 10 minutes of machine time. Average run time is roughly proportional to the total number of trees in the stand. Time differences between simulations of same-size stands are due primarily to random variations in the number of stand years during which beetles migrate into the stand.

- In principle there is no limit on stand size. However, practical limitations on the amount of output storage space, and on the time required for simulation, argue against large stands. For instance, each independent simulation of a 2-acre stand harvested at age 35 requires an average of 3 to 5 minutes, so a similar 10-acre stand would run an average of 15 to 25 minutes per independent replication.

- Due to large random fluctuations that occur between individual repetitions within simulations, model comparisons of management strategies (e.g., clonal plantings vs. those generated from seedlings or, in clonally generated stands, block plantings vs. random mix of ramets) should not be based on single stand simulations, but rather on multiple, independent replicates of any proposed strategy (we recommend 200 or more reps of each scenario of interest). Single stand simulations can, however, yield useful insights into beetle activities and their consequences as a stand ages.

B. The Simulations Themselves—What Output Information Is Saved

As described, table 1 enables us to use a single configuration number to represent the list of 11 stand parameters corresponding to an individual simulation. Together with table 3, it also indicates the overall plan for the simulations themselves: each simulation group is uniquely determined by its configuration number and the lines used from **input.txt**.

Following this format for identifying simulation inputs, the code saves output from each stand simulation in two files that are automatically created and placed in the folder **multiple**. The first of these, identified by "t", followed by the simulation number (line # from **input.txt**), stores information about each individual tree in the simulated stand. The second output file, labeled "s", followed by the simulation number, contains yearly summaries about the stand. These outputs include all the information that appears on your screen (section A.4) plus several additional entries. Here are the details:

B.1. The Tree-Information Output Files

For each stand simulation, a "t-file" is produced at harvest time. In this file, each row contains 11 entries that correspond to a particular tree in the simulation. These entries appear in the sequence:

$$[\text{pattern, seed pair, i, j, r0(i,j), g0(i,j), clntyp(i,j), yrdied(i,j),}$$
$$\text{daydied(i,j), lightning(i,j), vmerch(i,j)}]$$

where

pattern = the pattern in which stand trees are deployed (one of the entries in the second column of table 1)

seed pair = the **line number** used from the file **input.txt**

i = the tree's **row number** in the simulated stand

j = the **column number** of the tree

$r0(i,j)$ = constitutive **resin flow rate** (including site effect) for tree(i,j)

$g0(i,j)$ = **growth rate** (including site effect) assigned to tree(i,j)

clntyp(i,j) = **number of the clone** to which tree(i,j) belongs (= 0 if clones are not used in this simulation)

yrdied(i,j) = **stand age** (years) at which tree(i,j) died (= 0 if tree is still alive at harvest)

daydied(i,j) = **day of year** (1 = Jan 1; 365 = Dec 31) on which tree(i,j) died (= 0 if tree died from competition or is still alive at harvest)

lightning(i,j) = **cause of death** of tree(i,j) (see notes)

vmerch(i,j) = **merchantable volume** (cubic feet) of tree(i,j) (= 0 if the tree is dead)

Notes Related to the Tree-Information Files:

- In a "t-file", each row consists of data generated for a single tree. If a stand configuration is chosen from table 1, a row contains 11 entries.
- Values of **r0**, **g0** and **clntyp** are assigned at the beginning of the simulation and constitute part of the stand initialization. On the other hand, entries in **yrdied**, **daydied**, and **lightning** are determined as the daily simulation computations proceed, and are not known for all trees until the simulation terminates.
- Values of **yrdied, daydied, and lightning** contain more information than is at first apparent. For instance, **yrdied(i,j)** = 0 only if tree(i,j) is still alive at time of harvest, **yrdied(i,j)** = 8 indicates a tree that died during the 8-year tree juvenile period during which no beetles were present in the stand, and **yrdied(i,j)** = k > 8 means that tree(i,j) died during stand year k.
- Moreover, **daydied(i,j)** > 0 if tree(i,j) was killed by beetle penetrations **and/or** by lightning. For example, (**yrdied(i,j)** = 21, **daydied(i,j)** = 154, **lightning(i,j)** = 16) means tree(i,j) was killed by beetles *and* by lightning—on day 154 (June 3) of stand year 21, 16 days after being struck. On the other hand, (**yrdied(i,j)** = 21, **daydied(i,j)** = 154, **lightning(i,j)** = 30) means the tree was killed by lightning alone, while (**yrdied(i,j)** = 21, **daydied(i,j)** = 0) means that tree(i,j) died from tree competition at the beginning of year 21, prior to that year's daily updates, and was not killed by beetles.
- To clarify further the information supplied by the "lightning" matrix, **lightning(i,j)** = 0 if tree(i,j) was never struck by lightning during the entire course of the simulation; **lightning(i,j)** = n, where 0 < n < 30, if tree(i,j) *was* struck by lightning, then died n days later as a consequence of beetle attacks; and **lightning(i,j)** = 30 means the tree was struck by lightning, not killed by beetles during the following 30 days, and died (by default in the code) due to the original lightning strike.
- In short, from values of **yrdied, daydied,** and **lightning** we can determine *when* (year and day) and *why* (competition, lightning, beetles) each tree died, if at all. The possibilities are:

  yrdied(i,j) indicates the year of death, if any; **yrdied(i,j)** = 0 if tree(i,j) survives until harvest

  If tree(i,j) dies, then **yrdied(i,j)** > 0; in this case,
    - **daydied(i,j)** = 0 means tree(i,j) was killed by competition
    - **daydied(i,j)** > 0, **lightning(i,j)** = 0 means killed by beetles, not lightning

- **daydied(i,j)** > 0, **lightning(i,j)** = n (0 < n < 30) means killed by beetles and lightning
- **daydied(i,j)** > 0, **lightning(i,j)** = 30 means killed by lightning, not beetles

B.2. The Stand-Information Output Files

A "s-file" is created at the beginning of each simulation, and information is added to this file at the end of each simulated year. Each row in the file contains 19 entries that correspond to a particular clone, in a particular year, from year 8 until harvest. These entries are arranged in the sequence:

[pattern, seed pair, age, immi, clone #, %treesurv, %treekill_B, %treekill_L, %treekill_C, avdiam_surv, avdiam_KB, avdiam_KC, avhgt_surv, avhgt_KB, avhgt_KC, avres_surv, avres_KB, merchvol, basal_area]

where **pattern** and **seed pair** are as indicated above, and

age = stand age in years
immi = 1 if there was beetle immigration this year, and = 0 if no immigration
clone # = identification number of the clone about which info is reported (0 = entire stand)
%treesurv = for each clone, the percentage of planted trees that still survive
%treekill_B = for each clone, the percentage of planted trees killed by beetles *this* year
%treekill_L = for each clone, the percentage of planted trees killed by lightning *this* year
%treekill_C = for each clone, the percentage of planted trees killed by competition *this* year
avdiam_surv = for each clone, the average diameter (inches) for surviving trees
avdiam_KB = for each clone, the average diameter (inches) for trees killed by beetles *this* year (** see the first note)
avdiam_KC = for each clone, the average diameter (inches) for trees killed by competition *this* year (**)
avhgt_surv = for each clone, the average height (feet) for surviving trees
avhgt_KB = for each clone, the average height (feet) for trees killed by beetles *this* year (**)
avhgt_KC = for each clone, the average height (feet) for trees killed by competition *this* year (**)
avres_surv = for each clone, the average resin flow (g/24h from a 1.27 cm diameter wound) for surviving trees
avres_KB = for each clone, the average resin flow (g/24h) in trees killed by beetles up to the present
merchvol = for each clone, the total merchantable timber volume (cubic feet per acre planted) in its surviving trees
basal_area = for each clone, the basal area (square feet per acre planted) in its surviving trees

Notes Related to Stand-Information Files:

- Items marked by (**) differ from other closely related items in that they report on the current year, rather than being cumulative from time of stand planting. This is because heights and diameters of killed trees can be meaningfully compared to those of surviving trees only within the year of death.

- In each "s-file", in each year from age 8 to harvest, there is a line for each clone. With an average of 15 lines (1 + # of clones) per year, and harvest time of 35 years, an average "s-file" would contain about 15 x 28 = 420 lines, each with 19 entries.

- In the code, although competition deaths, tree diameters, and tree heights are computed at the beginning of each year, all information recorded in "s-files" is current as of the end of each year, in order to also take account of the year's tree mortality due to beetles.

- The four percentages listed can total more than 100. The reason is that trees can be killed by both beetles and lightning (in the code, this occurs when a lightning struck tree is subsequently killed by beetles before the default 30-day period ends; see the fourth note related to the "t-files").

- Juvenile tree deaths are listed in addition to those due to beetles, competition, and lightning in order for the percentages to include all planted trees.

- The merchantable volume in the stand is the sum of volumes of all *surviving* trees, computed on a per acre basis. For an individual clone, the same computation is made, though here the divisor used is the area occupied by the originally planted ramets of *that* clone, not the area of the entire stand.

- The basal area in the stand is the sum of all the cross-sectional areas of the surviving trees, computed on a per acre basis. For an individual clone, the same computation is made, though here the divisor used is the area occupied by the originally planted ramets of *that* clone, not the area of the entire stand.

- **Warning**: When clonal ramets are randomly mixed before planting, relative magnitudes of the per-acre volumes or basal areas reported may, due to chance proximity of clones with different growth rates, not reflect true comparisons of volumes these clones would produce if planted in individual blocks.

V. THE SPBLOB MODEL SOURCE CODE, WITH EMPHASIS ON PARAMETERS, THEIR VALUES, AND THEIR EFFECTS ON MODEL OUTPUT

A. Introduction

This chapter is offered for those users who want to tailor **SPBLOB** to their own uses. It explains the principal computations in the **SPBLOB** source code, and describes the major parameters, their values, and their sources in the literature. More detailed descriptions of a few particularly complex computations can be found in the folder **SPBLOB_Supporting_Info_re_Params_Values**, available at **www.srs. fs.usda.gov/idip/**. This folder will hereinafter be referred to as the **Supporting Information** folder.

Before continuing here, you may find it helpful to review chapter II, which contains an overview of the **SPBLOB** code and provides a descriptive summary of each of the major subroutines.

A.1. The SPBLOB Source Code

The **Source Code** is written primarily in Fortran with, as indicated, a few random number generators in C. If you want to create your own version of this code, begin by downloading a copy from **www.srs.fs.usda.gov/idip/**.

This code is in the form of a folder, called **spblob_11_27_2007** (updated versions will have later dates), in which individual files constitute the subroutines, functions, etc. that are necessary for compiling and running the code. In addition to these files, this folder contains the **interactive** and **multiple** subfolders that constitute the executable versions of the **SPBLOB** code described in chapters III and IV. Properly speaking, these subfolders are not part of the source code. Rather, the executable 'tree' programs they contain have been created from it.

A.1.1. Modifying and Recompiling the Source Code

One way to modify the source code is to open the relevant subroutine files and make the desired changes, editing them as you would any text file. After making your changes, if you want to re-build the executable **Interactive** code, set the variable "**batch**" in the subroutine **MAIN** to "0". To build the executable **Multiple** simulation version, set "**batch**" equal to "1". After recompiling either code, **be sure** to move the new "**tree**" file the computer compiler creates into the appropriate subfolder (**interactive**, if batch = 0, and **multiple**, if batch = 1) to replace the previous version of "**tree.exe**".

Various Fortran compilers are available in the public domain, and you may have your own favorite. (For instance, users of Unix/Linux compilers will probably create a Makefile for the project.) We used the **Open Watcom** compiler, which can be downloaded from **http://www.openwatcom.org**.

The current **Open Watcom** compiler (February 2008) version is 1.6, released in December, 2006. Two installation files are required, one for C/C++ and one for Fortran, since we use both languages in the **SPBLOB** code. Instructions for downloading and installing these compilers can be found in appendix A of this documentation.

If you apply the **Open Watcom** compiler software to open the project file **tree.wpj** it creates, you find three types of source files (other compilers may build different components):

- Fortran source code (for which subroutine names end with **.for**)
- C source code (ending with **.c**)
- Compiled lib files (ending with **.lib**)

The Fortran source codes are the major simulation subroutines. Several of these require generation of random values from uniform, gamma, normal, and/ or exponential probability distributions. For this purpose, we include in the code folder the random number generator library that can be downloaded from **http://biostatistics.mdanderson.org/SoftwareDownload/SingleSoftware. aspx?Software_Id=27**.

For us, some features of the Fortran version of this library did not work as expected, and we used the C version instead. To call the random number generator library in C source code requires use of the '$pragma' syntax to let the **Open Watcom** compiler know that some routines called by the Fortran codes are written in C. If you use a compiler other than **Open Watcom**, the '$pragma' syntax probably will need to be changed to fit your compiler's requirements. On the other hand, if you use the Fortran version of the random number library indicated, the '$pragma' syntax is not needed.

For example, the subroutines **'get_command_argument'** and **'command_ argument_count'**, which are called in subroutine **MAIN**, are subroutines from the lib file **f2kcli.lib**. The source file for this lib file, along with different binary versions for different operating systems and compilers, can be downloaded from **http://www. winteracter.com/f2kcli**.

If you use this library with a different compiler than **Open Watcom**, consult the **f2kcli** website for information concerning the proper documents to download. In **SPBLOB**, this library is used to interpret and act on command lines such as 'tree 1' ('1' is a command line parameter—a 'configuration' in **SPBLOB** terminology; see section IV.A.1). For some compilers this library may not be necessary since they may already include similar functions.

A.2. SPBLOB Parameters: Values, Sources, and Effects on Model Output

Symbols used in the **SPBLOB** code are either variables, parameters, or constants:

Variable—A quantity that can change over the course of a simulation
Parameter—A quantity that does not change value within a particular simulation of a particular stand, but may change from one simulation to another
Constant—A quantity that has the same numerical value in all model simulations

Most variables and parameters are numerical, but a few are logical quantities.

Parameters serve to clarify and give flexibility to the model code, and to calibrate simulation output. Most of the parameter values used in **SPBLOB** were obtained from field studies reported in the literature. Values not available from published sources were chosen to match model output as closely as possible to field observations. The **Glossary** in chapter VII contains definitions of all the important terms, including parameters. Here, we focus on sources from which the principal parameter values were obtained and, for those parameters for which values were not available directly, the methods used for their computation.

B. Parameters Associated with Stand Planting

As noted in section II.C.2, in **SPBLOB** a 'tree' is a pair of parameters that govern tree interactions with their neighbors and with their environment. These fundamental **SPBLOB** parameters are:

- **g0**—the tree's growth rate, a combination of genetic factors and site effects associated with the particular tree location at which it is planted. During simulation, this value, together with the **g0** values assigned to the tree's neighbors, controls the tree's survival and growth in the face of intrastand competition.
- **r0**—the tree's constitutive resin flow rate, which is the result of genetic and environmental factors. The value for **r0** governs the tree's success in repelling beetle attacks.

B.1. The Parameter g0

All **g0** values are assigned in subroutine **DEPLOY**, then used in subroutine **JUVEN** (Burkhart and others 1987; also see chapter II) as the stand advances through its 8-year juvenile growth stage. These values also play a central role in subroutines **COMP2** and **GROW2** (derived from Burkhart and others 1987) that govern the competitive yearly survival and growth of individual trees.

If clones are not used in establishing the stand, tree seedlings are generated randomly and independently from improved stock, their **g0** values coming from a normal distribution having mean 80.0 (average tree height, in feet, at age 25) and standard deviation 5.0. These values were chosen to represent tree growth on a site of moderately high productivity (Schultz 1997).

If clones *are* to be used, the **g0** values can be assigned by the user, if desired. When clone values are not assigned, the code censors the above Normal(80,25) distribution by accepting only those **g0** values that come from the upper 15 percent of the distribution, these censored values being independently assigned to clones. For each particular clone, all ramets are assigned the same genotypic **g0** value, whether these ramets are deployed together in blocks or are randomly mixed with those of other clones. An environmental effect is added to each value as the ramets are planted.

B.2. The Parameter r0

Based on a large-scale study of resin flow distributions (Roberds and others 2003), we assume that **r0** values follow a gamma distribution with parameters $\alpha = 2.5$ and $\beta = 0.6$. (Equivalently, the mean of **r0** is $\alpha\beta = 1.5$ while the standard deviation is $\mathrm{sqrt}(\alpha\beta^2) \cong 0.95$.) The units for **r0** are g/24h from a wound 1.27 cm in diameter. This distribution is used whether or not the stand is generated from clonal materials.

Predicated on results reported in Roberds and others (2003), we assume in assigning **r0** values to seedlings or clonal ramets, that **r0** and **g0** values are positively correlated, with correlation coefficient $\rho = 0.25$. Each **g0** value is assigned first, after which the code calls subroutine **CORRELATE** to determine the mean and variance of the gamma distribution from which the corresponding **r0** will be chosen. Subroutine **CLONE** then randomly chooses an **r0** value from this distribution. Full details of this computational process appear in the file **spblob_params_g0&r0.doc**, contained in the **Supporting Information** folder (see section A).

B.3. Assignment of Phenotypic Values to Trees

Pairs of **g0** and **r0** values represent tree genotypes. Tree planting then results in phenotypic values that combine genetic influences with environmental effects associated with the site at which the tree is located. In code subroutine **DEPLOY**, we assign individual tree, broad-sense heritability (Balocchi and others 1993, Falconer and Mackay 1996, Roberds and others 2003) equal to hsqg0 = 0.4 (a value consistent with a modest level of within-site environmental variability in loblolly pine stands). Here, hsqg0 = g0var/(g0var + siteg0) is the proportion of phenotypic variation in growth rate attributable to genetic sources. To obtain a tree's phenotypic **g0**, we first solve this equation for the variance, siteg0, that is associated with environmental effects:

$$siteg0 = g0var*(1-hsqg0)/hsqg0,$$

then randomly sample a N(0,siteg0) distribution to generate a random environmental effect, E. Adding E to the genotypic **g0** value (section B.1) produces the new, phenotypic value representing the total growth rate of the tree. This value, usually dubbed the 'site index' of the tree, represents the expected (average) height, in feet, that the tree will attain by age 25.

Following the same procedure, the code computes a phenotypic value for **r0** by adding a random environmental effect to the genotypic value generated in section B.2, assuming hsqr0 = 0.6 (Roberds and others 2003).

B.4. Edge Effects

To diminish edge effects associated with small stands, subroutine **DEPLOY** augments the stand with four additional rows above and below and four columns on each side. For these border trees, **r0** and **g0** values are assigned in ways that match them with the trees situated on the edges of the stand proper. In particular, if parameters for the trees in the stand are generated randomly and independently from fixed distributions, the same procedure is used for the added trees. If trees in the stand are arranged in clonal blocks, each block situated on an edge of the stand is extended perpendicular to that edge through four more rows or columns of trees having the same pair of **g0** and **r0** values assigned to trees in the block. Corners are extended so the rectangular shape of the original stand is preserved. The augmented stand is then simulated. However, all reported code outputs relating to trees (percent survival, numbers killed by beetles, total merchantable volume at harvest, etc.) or to beetle populations (average number of penetrations per attacked tree, average brood success, etc.) pertain only to the original stand.

C. Parameters Associated with Beetle Population Dynamics

Once the stand is planted, most of the code computation is related to changes that occur within beetle populations, and the effects that these changes have on trees in the stand.

C.1. Computation of SPB Vital Rates— Subroutine PARBTL

While SPB vital rates are influenced by a variety of external factors, the most important of these is temperature (Coulson 1980, Payne 1980, Stephen and Lih 1985, Ungerer and others 1999, Wagner and others 1984a, Wagner and others 1984b). In **SPBLOB** simulations, prior to commencement of yearly and daily updates of beetle populations, subroutine **PARBTL** computes these rates as functions of temperature, using formulas described in Wagner and others (1984a) and Ungerer and others (1999). These temperature-dependent functions fall into two categories. The first computes the per-day parent female oviposition rate, as a proportion of the average total number of eggs a female parent deposits while in a tree, if temperature were to remain constant throughout the day. Formulas in the second category compute the proportion of total development within each juvenile life stage (egg, larva, pupa, preadult) that would accrue over the course of a day, again assuming temperature remains constant throughout the day. For each temperature from 1 °C to 45 °C, values of these five rates are stored in matrix **devrat**, to be used throughout the remainder of the simulation (in particular, see sections G and J).

C.2. Beetle Immigration and Emigration

To some extent loblolly plantations have low-level, endemic beetle populations, even in absence of infestations that kill trees. These beetles can result from chance events such as wind-blown arrival from infested stands, but appear primarily to be associated with weakened and lightning-struck trees within the stand (see, e.g., Blanche and others (1983) and references therein). Occasionally, favorable weather or high immigration will initiate stand infestations with enough beetles to kill healthy trees, the progeny spreading to nearby trees and creating the 'spots' of dead trees familiar in infested stands.

C.2.1. Immigration
In the Southeastern United States, beetle populations in a stand are expected to increase to outbreak levels about once in 25 to 30 years, on average (Personal communication. 2007. James Meeker, Entomologist, USDA Forest Service-FHP, 2500 Shreveport Highway, Pineville, LA 71360). Based on this observation, **SPBLOB** models the immigration process as a Markov chain (Bishir and others 2004) having a probability of approximately 0.03 of occurring in any given year. In years when immigration occurs, the per day rate of beetle arrival to the *stand* is modeled as:

$$avimmi = parimmi*wintersurv*ntrees*exp(-(y**2)/2)$$

where

parimmi = calibration parameter
wintersurv = probability an adult beetle survived the preceding winter's coldest temperatures
ntrees = number of live trees in the stand
y = (nday - 110)/50
nday = day number during the year (January 1 is day 1, etc.)

In the simulation code, the default value of parimmi is 0.0875, chosen so that model simulations produce 'spot' activity that approximates levels observed in the field. (As is the case for all parameters, this value—assigned in subroutine **SIMUL**—can be modified by the user.)

C.2.2. Emigration
Beetle departure from the stand is possible whenever SPB are present in the stand, not just during immigration years, and is modeled in a similar way to immigration. Here, the probability that an *individual* beetle leaves the stand during a particular update period (these occur four times per day) is:

$$premi = paremi* exp(-(y**2)/2)/(1.0 + (yrnum/15.0)**4)$$

where

paremi = calibration parameter
yrnum = stand age in years
y = (nday - 110)/50
nday = day number during the year (January 1 is day 1, etc.)

The default value of paremi is 0.001, leading to a maximum per-beetle departure probability, per update period, of 0.00088 (about 1 beetle in 1,130) in year 9, declining to 0.000033 (about 1 beetle in 30,000) per update period in year 35. At these rates, the probability a beetle in a 9 year old stand would leave *sometime* during the year is about 0.5, a figure that drops to about 0.02 at stand age 35. The exit probability decreases as the stand matures because beetles prefer taller, denser, and older stands of loblolly pine (Belanger and others 1993, Coster and Searcy 1981).

Beetle migration itself is computed in subroutine **DISPERSE**, departing beetles being a portion of the dispersing group, while immigrants are added to those beetles that will constitute the 'landed' category in the next update period (see section L).

D. Simulation of Temperatures

In Southeastern United States, the region of interest in this study, daily long-term average temperatures over the course of the year roughly follow a sine curve, the lowest point occurring about January 20 and the highest about July 20. Such a curve is completely determined by TMEAN, the overall yearly average, and TDEV, the difference between the average for July 20 and the yearly average, TMEAN. Typically, these parameters are set by the user. For any particular location, these two quantities can be found by going to **www.noaa.gov** and clicking on NOAA Climate Data at a Glance. Once these parameters are specified, the code will compute the long-term average for each particular day in a simulation.

Actual daily averages can vary considerably from the corresponding long-term averages. Also, successive daily readings tend to be positively correlated (e.g., if one day is warmer than average, the next tends to be also). In the **SPBLOB** code, these aspects of daily temperatures are modeled in two steps:

(1) (Correlation) $av(n) = [av(n-1) + long(n)]/2$

where

av(n) = 'expected' average temperature on day n
av(n -1) = average observed temperature on day n-1
long(n) = long-term average temperature for day n

(2) (Randomization) The simulated 'actual' average, high, and low temperatures on day n are generated using normal distributions centered at av(n)

Once the average and high temperatures are known for the day, temperatures over the course of that day can then be approximated by another sine curve (Baskerville and Emin 1969). In **SPBLOB**, we use subroutine **TEMP** to compute these temperatures every 3 hours, then read corresponding temperature-dependent SPB rates from matrix **devrat** (section C.1) for each 3-hour period, assuming a constant temperature level over the period.

E. Frequency of Lightning Strikes

Lightning plays an important role in the loblolly pine/southern pine beetle system. For instance, Hodges and Pickard (1971) estimate that 31 percent of the spots that occur in loblolly stands originate in lightning-struck trees. In **SPBLOB**, Coulson and others (1983) is followed in modeling the average number of thunderstorms on each day during the year as a multiple of a normal density having mean 220 and standard deviation of 60. Since day number 220 is August 8, this means that storm activity is highest in early August, although storms are common over most of the summer and fall seasons. The multiplier depends on the geographic location, being highest in Florida and diminishing as we move north (Coulson and others 1983, fig. 2). A multiplier of 60, for example, results in an average of about 50 storms per year. Assuming 2 strikes per square mile, per storm (Coulson and others 1983, p. 186), we estimate that a stand planted using 3-m spacing and having 32 rows and columns (about 2.28 acres, or 0.9 ha) would experience about 12 strikes between ages 9 and 35 years, the default simulation period in **SPBLOB**. More extensive computational details appear in the file **spblob_params_lightning.doc**, contained in the **Supporting Information** folder.

F. Beetle Mortality Due to Extremely Cold Temperatures

Following Ungerer and others (1999) beetle mortality engendered by cold temperatures is modeled in subroutine **COLD** using normal distributions. Suppose X is a normal random variable with mean μ and standard deviation σ. In model simulations, if a day's simulated minimum temperature, tmin, is less than -2 °C, then:

- Adult landed and parent beetles (see section II.E.4, page 9) independently survive with probability Pr(X < tmin), where μ = -12.9 °C and σ = 2.9 °C

- Eggs and larvae survive independently with probability Pr(X < tmin), where μ = -11.5 °C and σ = 2.91 °C

- Pupae survive independently with probability Pr(X < tmin), where μ = -9.8 °C and σ = 2.6 °C

For example, a single overnight low temperature of -15 °C (regardless of duration) kills about 77 percent of adults, 88 percent of larvae and almost 98 percent of the pupae in each tree. Beetle mortality levels of this magnitude can significantly decrease the potential for tree damage in the following year.

G. Juvenile Development and Mortality over the Course of a Day

In addition to the special beetle mortality discussed in section F, there is mortality associated with all beetle activities. The remainder of this section discusses juvenile development as well as mortality, while adult mortalities are the subjects of sections J.3 and L.

For each juvenile life stage, subroutine **UPDATE** starts with the temperatures generated every 3 hours by subroutine **TEMP**, reads from matrix **devrat** (sections C.1 and D)—for that life stage—the per-day development proportion corresponding to each of these eight temperatures, multiplies each proportion by 1/8 to convert to a 3-hour basis, and sums values for the eight proportions to obtain the proportion of total development in that life stage during the day. Subroutine **ENDOFDAY** (sections I and J) then checks the current life stage of each juvenile cohort and adds today's additional proportion to the proportion already accumulated. If the new proportion is < 1.0, the cohort remains in the same stage. Otherwise, the code moves the cohort to the next stage, and assigns its state of maturity in the new stage as the accumulated proportion in the preceding stage, less 1.0.

The code then assesses the proportion of beetle natural mortality in each stage, over and above that due to cold temperatures. Following Coulson and others (1977), Fargo and others (1979) and Coulson (1980, figs. 5-8 and 5-9), it applies a constant survival rate of 0.98 per 1 percent of **total** (egg to maturity) development, a figure chosen to result in a number of brood adults totaling about 13 percent of the original number of new eggs. In addition, based on Thatcher (1967), additional larval mortality is assigned on unusually hot days. Details concerning both these computations appear in the file **spblob_params_SPB_natural_mort.doc** contained in the **Supporting Information** folder.

H. The Process of Beetle Attack on Trees—Subroutine ATTACK

To reproduce, female SPB must successfully penetrate the bark of a tree, mate, create egg galleries in the cambium, and oviposit. These activities require that the tree's ability to repel an attack be overcome. The code models this reproductive process in successive steps:

- If a live tree has been struck by lightning, the probability that an arriving beetle attacks is 1.0 (that is, all landed beetles attack)
- Otherwise, the probability a landed beetle attacks is equal to the larger of

$$p1 = (0.37 - 0.345*\exp(-RATK6*phrpos))*\exp(-RATK3*phrneg)$$

and

$$R = (npen/bole)/100$$

where

exp denotes the exponential function
phrpos = concentration of positive pheromones near the tree
phrneg = concentration of negative pheromones near the tree
npen = current total number of penetrations of the tree
bole = tree bole area, in square meters

Because successful beetle reproduction depends on tree death, this form for R is based on an assumption that beetles are more likely to attack as tree death approaches. The values of parameters RATK6 and RATK3 are set in subroutine **ATTACK**, being chosen so that average levels of tree mortality seen in code simulations seem reasonable. As more information becomes available, it can be incorporated as desired.

The probability that an attacking beetle successfully penetrates to the cambium depends on the tree's resin flow rate, and is modeled as:

$$prob = 0.94/(1.0 + (resin(i,j)/ratk50)^m)$$

the values ratk50 = 2.3 and m = 2 being chosen to reflect experimental observations, primarily Hodges and others (1979). Details are in the file **spblob_params_SPB_attack_success.doc** contained in the **Supporting Information** folder. The numerator value 0.94 derives from the observation in Bunt and others (1980) that 6 percent of beetles landing on a tree during mass attack succumbed to predators.

I. Tree Response to Beetle Attack— Subroutine ENDOFDAY

Trees defend themselves from SPB primarily by exuding resin at attack sites on the bole. Trees with sufficient resin 'pitch out' beetles attempting to enter. Those with naturally low resin flow rates, and others that have low resin due to lightning strikes or drought, are more susceptible to attack and often serve as initiation points for spot formation (Gara and others 1965, Hodges and Pickard 1971).

I.1. Resin Loss from Flow through Attack Holes

In the code, trees that have been attacked by beetles but that have not been struck by lightning, lose resin at a rate proportional to both the number of active penetration holes, per unit bole area, and the tree's current resin level, according to the formula:

$$new\_resin\_level = previous\_level*(1.0 - 0.00186*natk/bole)$$

where

  natk = total number of penetration holes through which resin is flowing
  bole = total bole area of the tree

The multiplier 0.00186 represents an average resin flow rate (g/24h) per active penetration hole. Resistant trees respond rapidly to this loss by producing new resin (Ruel and others 1998). However, any tree can be overcome by a sufficiently large number of beetle attacks.

Lightning-struck trees are modeled differently, in that there is no resin replenishment. Such trees are highly susceptible to beetle attack and may be quickly located by foraging SPB. Following Hodges and Pickard (1971), who reported flow rates in struck trees being only 5 to15 percent of those in similar control trees, we model tree resin level as:

$$new\_resin\_level = 0.905*previous\_level$$

The multiplier 0.905 leads to a 95 percent loss of tree resin within 30 days.

I.2. Tree Mortality Due to Beetle Penetrations

Based on Hodges and others (1979) and Fargo and others (1978), we assume that the *average* number of beetle penetrations per square meter of bole area, required to kill a tree is numerically equal to 64*sqrt(RMAX), where RMAX is the tree's maximum resin flow rate 'this year.' (RMAX is measured as g/24h from a 1.27 cm hole.) The multiplier, 64, carries units that transform the above formula into number of penetrations.

In the code, the actual number of penetrations needed in any particular tree is modeled as a normal random variable having mean $\mu = 64*sqrt(RMAX)$ and standard deviation $\sigma = 6.4*sqrt(RMAX)$. Thus, for example, the probability equals $Pr(W \leq 70) = 0.8258$ that no more than 70 penetrations, per square meter of bole area, are required to kill a tree having resin flow value RMAX = 1.0.

Daily code computations proceed as in the following example (readers whose probability theory is rusty may prefer to skip this).

Example: Suppose that in preceding days, a surviving tree T with inherent resin flow value RMAX =1.0, has already suffered a total of x successful penetrations per unit bole area. If by today's end the new total is y, then

$$Pr(T \text{ dies today}) = Pr(W \le y \mid W > x) = Pr(x < W \le y)/Pr(W > x)$$

For instance, if x = 64 and y = 70, then

$$Pr(T \text{ dies today}) = Pr(64 < W \le 70)/Pr(W > 64)$$
$$= (0.8258 - 0.5)/0.5 = 0.6516$$

For a more general discussion, go to the **Supporting Information** folder and consult the files **spblob_params_SPB_attack_success.doc** and **spblob_params_tree_mort_from_SPB.doc**.

Penetrations do not cease immediately upon tree death. Again following Hodges and others (1979) and Fargo and others (1978), in subroutine **ENDOFDAY** we continue penetrations for 10 additional days, or until the total number of penetrations deters further attacks, whichever comes first. (Consult the code for details.)

J. Activities of Parent Beetles—Subroutine ENDOFDAY (continued)

In **SPBLOB**, all parent beetle vital rates are directly or indirectly based on parameter values drawn from the literature (Ungerer and others 1999; Wagner and others 1984a).

J.1. *Proportion* of Her Total Eggs That a Female Parent Deposits in a Day

Starting with the temperatures generated every 3 hours by subroutine **TEMP**, subroutine **EGG** reads from array **devrat** (section C.1) the *daily* oviposition proportion corresponding to each temperature, multiplies this proportion by 1/8 to convert to a 3-hour basis, and sums values for the eight proportions to obtain **eggpro**, the *proportion* of the total egg production a parent female will deposit that day.

J.2. Total *Number* (newegg) of Eggs Laid in Each Tree

Coulson and others (1976) model the total egg gallery length that a single female parent creates during the course of her stay in a particular tree as a function of the density of parents presently in the tree. This relationship may be expressed as:

$$G = 66.41\exp(-0.245A)$$

where

G = average total gallery length (cm) created per female parent
A = average number of female parents per square meter of bole area
exp denotes the exponential function

Using the Foltz and others (1976) estimate that about 1.59 eggs are deposited per cm of gallery length, and replacing A by B = average number of female parents per square foot of bole area, the formula for G translates into:

$$TE = 105.6*\exp(-0.0264B)$$

where

TE = average total number of eggs a female will deposit in the tree

Since the code tracks only the female portion of the beetle population, we assume a 1:1 sex ratio (e.g., Bunt and others 1980, Coulson and others 1976) and approximate the total number of female eggs that ultimately will be deposited in the tree by ALL the parents now in the tree as:

$$nnnegg = int(0.5*PAR*TE)$$

where

PAR = total number of parents in the tree
the function int returns the largest integer less than or equal to its argument

Finally, on a particular day during which the egg proportion **eggpro** (section J.1) is deposited, the total number of new eggs deposited in the tree is:

$$newegg = bin(nnnegg, eggpro)$$

In words, newegg is a randomly generated value from a binomial distribution (a 'binomial deviate') with nnnegg 'trials' and per-trial 'success' probability equal to **eggpro**.

J.3. Daily Parent Survival and Reemergence

In apparent absence of *in vivo* observations of the SPB parent survival rate, the **SPBLOB** code approximates this rate indirectly, based on three facts:

- When a parent completes her oviposition in a tree, the cumulative proportion of her total egg complement deposited is 1.0
- Estimates of reemergence rates of parent SPB vary widely (Coulson 1980, p. 77), the average of these estimates being about 0.7
- Algebraically, exponents are added when products of exponential quantities are computed: e.g., $a^x a^y = a^{x+y}$

Following the observation in Gagne and others (1982, p. 1220) that "the pattern of oviposition rate . . . is surprisingly similar to the pattern of reemergence," we compute the proportion of parents that reemerge on a particular day as *equal* to **eggpro**, the proportion of her total eggs that a female deposits that day (section J.1). (This observation, and our application of it, are consistent with the supposition that parents reemerge *because* their oviposition is complete.) As a consequence, the total number of reemerging parents is computed as:

$$RE = bin(PAR, eggpro)$$

where, as in section J.2,
PAR = toal number of parents in the tree
bin denotes a binomial deviate

To ensure a reemergence rate consistent with the literature, we begin with the fact that the total probability a parent survives her stay in a tree is the product of the daily survival probabilities encountered along the way. Based on the three facts listed above, we therefore model the probability that a parent survives on a particular day as:

$$ps = 0.7^{eggpro}$$

The *definition* of **eggpro** (section J.1), implies that a surviving parent should reemerge when her **eggpro** values total 1.0. Thus, the formula for ps, together with fact # 3, produces a total survival probability (equivalently, a reemergence probability) of $0.7^{1.0} = 0.7$, consistent with the second fact.

Finally, we update the parent population itself using the formulas

$$NEWPAR = PAR - RE + PEN$$

$$NEWPAR = bin(NEWPAR, ps)$$

where

PAR, RE, ps, and bin are as above
NEWPAR = the new number of parents
PEN = the total number of successful penetrations by landed beetles today

K. Pheromone Production, Concentrations, and Diffusion

Female beetles that successfully penetrate the tree's inner bark emit pheromones that attract both sexes; this pheromone production ceases when bark penetration is complete (Payne 1980). In the model, each female that enters is joined by a male, and the two work to create galleries along which the female deposits eggs. Males that join successful females in a penetration hole emit pheromones that repel other beetles, an emission that continues throughout gallery construction and oviposition. The result is an attack process that initially increases in intensity, as more beetles are attracted to female pheromones, then diminishes as increasing numbers of males arrive (Payne 1980, Coulson 1980).

K.1. Production— Subroutines UPDATE and ENDOFDAY

In the code, positive and negative pheromone concentrations are updated each day. The formulas, which apply to each live tree, are:

newpos = RPHER1*PEN	[in **UPDATE**, four times per day]
newneg = RPHER2*nmale	[in **ENDOFDAY**]

where, for each particular tree

PEN = the number of attacking females that have successfully penetrated the tree's bark 'today'
nmale = the number of males (cumulative, up to the present) that have joined successful females in attack holes
newpos = the positive pheromone concentration resulting from female production
newneg = the negative pheromone concentration resulting from male production
RPHER1 and RPHER2 are the per individual productions from females and males, respectively

Because in the model, beetle movement depends only on *relative* pheromone concentrations on nearby trees (section L), values of parameters RPHER1 and RPHER2 are arbitrarily set equal to 1.0. (These parameters thus help clarify the structure of the model, but do not represent actual pheromone levels in the field.)

K.2. Diffusion and Resulting Concentrations— Subroutine DIFFUSE

The pheromone production streams, newpos and newneg, diffuse rapidly (in the model, within the same update period) through the stand, leading to adjusted concentrations that affect beetle attack and dispersal processes. The concentration of positive pheromone surrounding tree T is computed as:

$$pherpos(T) = newpos(T) + \Sigma\ newpos(B)*(((0.9)**m)/(8*m))$$

where

pherpos(T) = total concentration around tree T
newpos(B) = positive pheromone produced at tree B (K.1)
m = larger of the number of rows and the number of columns separating
the two trees

The sum extends over all trees in the stand, with the exception of tree T itself. The 'dissipation' rate 0.9 approximates measurements reported in Thistle and others (2004) and discussed in section II.E.5.2, while 8m is the number of trees located in the m-th ring of trees surrounding tree T. (A similar formula is used to compute the concentration of negative pheromone. See the **Source Code** for details.)

L. Beetle Dispersal—Subroutine DISPERSE

In the model, beetle dispersal from a tree is governed by the *relative* pheromone concentrations associated with trees that are adjacent to the source tree (section K.2). More precisely, in order to reproduce the compact 'spots' observed in attacked stands, the code moves all beetles that depart from a tree T to the tree adjacent to T that has the largest positive pheromone concentration.

Based on Coulson (1980) and Pope and others (1980), the temperature-dependent mortality rate, per day, experienced by dispersing beetles is modeled in subroutine **UPDATE** as:

$$DFLY = 0.03748 + 0.00562 * exp(0.11644 * avtemp)$$

where

avtemp = average temperature for the day

See the file **spblob_params_dispersal_mort.doc** in the **Supporting Information** folder for additional details.

M. Tree Decay and Fall—Subroutine SIMUL

In the code, trees that die, whether from competition, lightning, or beetle attack, are categorized as 'fallen' after being dead 5 years. The impact is to shift over to standing trees the beetle immigrants that otherwise would land on dead trees. (Here, 'land' is to be taken literally; beetles *never* attack dead trees, but leave at the first opportunity. Our usage follows Bunt and others (1980) who reported that beetles seem to be attracted by any large vertical object and ". . . often landed on the observer.")

N. Merchantable Volume—Subroutine OUTPUT

Beginning at stand age 9 years, and continuing until tree harvest, subroutine **OUTPUT** computes the total cubic foot volume of merchantable timber available in the stand. While the original version of this **PTAEDA** subroutine (Burkhart and others 1987, Daniels and Burkhart 1975) offers several choices for the meaning of 'merchantable,' **SPBLOB** reports only 'inside bark' volume of the portion of the tree bole between stump height and the upper point at which the diameter = 4 inches, taken from all live trees whose diameters exceed 4.5 inches (in **PTAEDA** notation, d.b.h. > 5.0). However, these default choices can be altered by the user if desired.

VI. LITERATURE CITED

Balocchi, C.E.; Bridgwater, F.E.; Zobel, B.J.; Jahromi, S. 1993. Age trends in genetic parameters for tree height in a nonselected population of loblolly pine. Forest Science. 39: 231-251.

Baskerville, G.L.; Emin, P. 1969. Rapid estimation of heat accumulation from maximum and minimum temperatures. Ecology. 50: 514-517.

Belanger, R.P.; Hedden, R.L.; Lorio, P.L., Jr. 1993. Management strategies to reduce losses from the southern pine beetle. Southern Journal of Applied Forestry. 17: 150-154.

Berryman, A.A. 1972. Resistance of conifers to invasion by bark beetle-fungus association. BioScience. 22: 598-602.

Bishir, J.; Roberds, J. 1995. Analysis of failure time in clonally propagated plant populations. Mathematical Biosciences. 125: 109-125.

Bishir, J.; Roberds, J. 1997. Limit theorems and a general framework for risk analysis in clonal forestry. Mathematical Biosciences. 142: 1-11.

Bishir, J.; Roberds, J.H. 1999. On numbers of clones needed for managing risks in clonal forestry. Forest Genetics. 6: 149-155.

Bishir, J.; Roberds, J.H.; Strom, B.L. 2004. On-bark behavior of *Dendroctonus frontalis*: a Markov chain analysis. Journal of Insect Behavior. 17: 281-301.

Blanche, C.A.; Hodges, J.D.; Nebeker, T.E.; Moehring, D.M. 1983. Southern pine beetle: the host dimension. Bulletin 917. Mississippi State, MS: Mississippi Agricultural and Forestry Experiment Station. 29 p.

Bunt, W.D.; Coster, J.E.; Johnson, P.C. 1980. Behavior of the southern pine beetle on the bark of host trees during mass attack. Annals of the Entomological Society of America. 73: 647-652.

Burkhart, H.E.; Farrar, K.D.; Amateis, R.L.; Daniels, R.F. 1987. Simulation of individual tree growth and development in loblolly pine plantations on cutover, site-prepared areas. Publ. No. FWS-1-87. Blacksburg, VA: Virginia Polytechnic Institute and State University, School of Forestry and Wildlife Resources. 47 p.

Coster, J.E.; Searcy, J.L. 1981. Site, stand, and host characteristics of southern pine beetle infestations. Tech. Bull. No. 1612. Washington, DC: U.S. Department of Agriculture Combined Forest Pest Research and Development Program. 115 p.

Coulson, R.N. 1980. Population dynamics. In: Thatcher, R.C.; Searcy, J.E.; Coster, J.E.; Hertel, G.D., eds. The Southern Pine Beetle. Tech. Bull. No. 1631. Washington, DC: U.S. Department of Agriculture Science and Technical Administration: 71-105.

Coulson, R.N.; Fargo, W.S.; Pulley, P.E. [and others]. 1978. Evaluation of the re-emergence process of parent adult *Dendroctonus frontalis* (Coleoptera: Scolytidae). Canadian Entomologist. 110: 475-486.

Coulson, R.N.; Feldman, R.M.; Sharpe, P.J.H. [and others]. 1989. An overview of the TAMBEETLE model of *Dendroctonus frontalis* population dynamics. Holarctic Ecology. 12: 445-450.

Coulson, R.N.; Hennier, P.B.; Flamm, R.O. [and others]. 1983. The role of lightning in the epidemiology of the Southern Pine Beetle. Zeitschrift fur Angewandte Entomologie. 96: 182-193.

Coulson, R.N.; Mayyasi, A.M.; Foltz, J.L. [and others]. 1976. Resource utilization by the southern pine beetle, *Dendroctonus frontalis* (Coleoptera: Scolytidae). Canadian Entomologist. 108: 353-362.

Coulson, R.N.; Pulley, P.E.; Foltz, J.L. [and others]. 1977. Survival models for within-tree populations of *Dendroctonus frontalis* (Coleoptera: Scolytidae). Canadian Entomologist. 109: 1071-1077.

Coyne, J.F.; Lott, L.H. 1976. Toxicity of substances in pine oleoresin to southern pine beetles. Journal of the Georgia Entomological Society. 11: 301-305.

Curry, G.L.; Feldman, R.M.; Smith, K.C. 1978. A stochastic model of a temperature-dependent population. Theoretical Population Biology. 13: 197-212.

Daniels, R.F.; Burkhart, H.E. 1975. Simulation of individual tree growth and stand development in managed loblolly pine plantations. Publ. No. FWS-5-75. Blacksburg, VA: Virginia Polytechnic Institute and State University, Division of Forestry and Wildlife Resources. 69 p.

Falconer, D.S.; Mackay, T.F.C. 1996. Introduction to Quantitative Genetics. 4th ed. Sussex, England: Longman Group Limited. 464 p.

Fargo, W.S.; Coulson, R.N.; Gagne, J.A.; Foltz, J.L. 1979. Correlation of southern pine beetle attack density, oviposition, and generation survival with host tree characteristics and preceeding beetle life stages within the host. Environmental Entomology. 8: 624-628.

Fargo, W.S.; Coulson, R.N.; Pulley, P.E. [and others]. 1978. Spatial and temporal patterns of within-tree colonization by *Dendroctonus frontalis* (Coleoptera: Scolytidae). Canadian Entomologist. 110: 1213-1232.

Foltz, J.L.; Mayyasi, A.M.; Hain, F.P. [and others]. 1976. Egg-gallery length relationship and within-tree analyses for the southern pine beetle, *Dendroctonus frontalis* (Coleoptera: Scolytidae). Canadian Entomologist. 108: 341-352.

Gagne, J.A.; Wagner, T.L.; Sharpe, P.J.H. [and others]. 1982. Reemergence of *Dendroctonus frontalis* (Coleoptera: Scolytidae) at constant temperatures. Environmental Entomology. 11: 1216-1222.

Gara, R.L.; Vité, J.P.; Cramer, H.H. 1965. Manipulation of *Dendroctonus frontalis* by use of a population aggregating pheromone. Contributions from Boyce Thompson Institute for Plant Research. 23: 55-66.

Hodges, J.D.; Elam, W.W.; Watson, W.F.; Nebeker, T.E. 1979. Oleoresin characteristics and susceptibility of four southern pines to southern pine beetle (Coleoptera: Scolytidae) attacks. Canadian Entomologist. 111: 889-896.

Hodges, J.D.; Pickard, L.S. 1971. Lightning in the ecology of the southern pine beetle, *Dendroctonus frontalis* (Coleoptera: Scolytidae). Canadian Entomologist. 103: 44-51.

Libby, W.J. 1982. What is a safe number of clones? In: Resistance to Disease and Pests in Forest Trees. Heybroek, H.; Stephan, B.; von Weissenberg, K., eds. Proceedings of the 3rd International Workshop on the Genetics of Host-Parasite Interactions in Forestry. Wageningen, The Netherlands, Sept. 1980: 342-360.

Lih, M.P.; Stephen, F.M.; Jeng, K.J. 1995. *SPBMODEL A User's Guide*. Offprint, Department of Entomology, Fayetteville, AR: University of Arkansas.

Lorio, P.L., Jr. 1986. Growth-differentiation balance: a basis for understanding southern pine beetle-tree interactions. Forest Ecology and Management. 14: 259-273.

Lorio, P.L., Jr.; Sommers, R.A.; Blanche, C.A. [and others]. 1990. Modeling pine resistance to bark beetles based on growth and differentiation balance principles. In: Dixon, R.K.; Meldahl, R.S.; Ruark, G.A.; Warren, W.G., eds. Process Modeling of Forest Growth Responses to Environmental Stress. Portland, OR: Timber Press: 402-409.

Muhs, H.-J. 1993. Policies, regulations and laws affecting clonal forestry. In: Ahuja, M.; Libby, W.J., eds. Clonal Forestry. Springer-Verlag: 215-227. Vol. 2.

Payne, T.L. 1980. Life history and habits. In: Thatcher, R.C.; Searcy, J.E.; Coster, J.E.; Hertel, G.D., eds. The Southern Pine Beetle. Tech. Bull. No. 1631. Washington, DC: U.S. Department of Agriculture Science and Technical Administration: 7-28.

Pope, D.N.; Coulson, R.N.; Fargo, W.S. [and others]. 1980. The allocation process and between-tree survival probabilities in *Dendroctonus frontalis* infestations. Researches in Population Ecology. 22: 197-210.

Roberds, J.H.; Bishir, J. 1997. Risk analyses in clonal forestry. Canadian Journal of Forest Research. 27: 425-432.

Roberds, J.H.; Namkoong, G.; Skroppa, T. 1990. Genetic analysis of risk in clonal populations of forest trees. Theoretical and Applied Genetics. 79: 841-848.

Roberds, J.H.; Strom, B.L.; Hain, F.P. [and others]. 2003. Estimates of genetic parameters for oleoresin and growth traits in juvenile loblolly pine. Canadian Journal of Forest Research. 33: 2469-2476.

Ruel, J.J.; Ayres, M.P.; Lorio, P.L., Jr. 1998. Loblolly pine responds to mechanical wounding with increased resin flow. Canadian Journal of Forest Research. 28: 596-602.

Schultz, R.P. 1997. Loblolly pine: the ecology and culture of loblolly pine (*Pinus taeda* L.). Agric. Handb. 713. Washington, DC.: U.S. Department of Agriculture. 12 chapters + Appendices.

Sharpe, P.J.H.; Curry, G.L.; DeMichele, D.W.; Cole, C.L. 1977. Distribution model of organism development times. Journal of Theoretical Biology. 66: 21-38.

Stephen, F.M.; Lih, M.P. 1985. A *Dendroctonus frontalis* infestation growth model: organization, refinement, and utilization. In: Branham, S.B.; Thatcher, R.C., eds. Integrated Pest Management Research Symposium: The Proceedings. Gen. Tech. Rep. SO-56. Asheville, NC: U.S. Department of Agriculture, Forest Service: 186-194.

Thatcher, R.C. 1967. Winter brood development of southern pine beetle in southeast Texas. Journal of Economic Entomology. 60: 599-600.

Thistle, H.W.; Peterson, H.; Allwine, G. [and others]. 2004. Surrogate pheromone plumes in three forest trunk spaces: composite statistics and case studies. Forest Science. 50: 610-625.

Ungerer, M.J.; Ayres, M.P.; Lombardero, M.J. 1999. Climate and the northern distribution limits of *Dendroctonus frontalis* Zimmermann (Coleoptera: Scolytidae). Journal of Biogeography. 26: 1133-1145.

Wagner, T.L.; Gagne, J.A.; Sharpe, P.J.H.; Coulson, R.N. 1984a. A biophysical model of southern pine beetle, *Dendroctonus frontalis* Zimmermann (Coleoptera: Scolytidae) development. Ecological Modelling. 21: 125-147.

Wagner, T.L.; Gagne, J.A.; Sharpe, P.J.H.; Coulson, R.N. 1984b. Effects of constant temperature on longevity of adult Southern Pine Beetles (Coleoptera: Scolytidae). Environmental Entomology. 13: 1125-1130.

VII. GLOSSARY FOR THE SPBLOB SOURCE CODE

In this glossary, **PTAEDA2** is the tree competition and growth code described in Daniels and Burkhart (1975) and Burkhart and others (1987), portions of which are incorporated by permission into **SPBLOB**. Also:

Constants are quantities whose values remain the same in all model simulations.

Parameters are quantities that do not change value within a particular simulation of a particular stand.

Variables are quantities that change over time within a particular simulation.

Most of these quantities are numerical, but a few have logical or character type.

---

acres: the number of acres in the simulated stand.

alpha: first parameter of a gamma distribution for resin flow that is correlated with a previously generated **g0** value (see **beta**).

alphares: first parameter of the gamma distribution for tree resin flow rates reported in Roberds and others (2003) (see **betares**).

amerch: average merchantable timber volume per live tree.

ampl: the deviation, on a particular day, between the simulated 'actual' average temperature for that day, and the simulated high (or low) temperature for the day.

avdeath: average number of penetrations, per square meter of bole area, needed to kill a tree. The actual number needed is modeled as a normal random variable.

avdiam: a vector, in which the k-th entry is the average diameter (inches) of all live trees of clone type k 'this' year.

avdiam_KB: a vector, in which the k-th entry is the average diameter (inches) of all trees of clone type k that were killed by beetles 'this' year.

avdiam_KC: a vector, in which the k-th entry is the average diameter (inches) of all trees of clone type k that were killed by competition 'this' year.

avhgt: a vector, in which the k-th entry is the average height (feet) of all live trees of clone type k 'this' year.

avhgt_KB: a vector, in which the k-th entry is the average height (feet) of all trees of clone type k that were killed by beetles 'this' year.

avhgt_KC: a vector, in which the k-th entry is the average height (feet) of all trees of clone type k that were killed by competition 'this' year.

avimmi: the average number of beetles, per (alive or dead) standing tree, that migrate into the stand on a particular day.

avres: a vector, in which the k-th entry is the average resin flow rate (gm/24h) of all live trees of clone type k 'this' year.

avres_KB: a vector, in which the k-th entry is the average resin flow rate of all trees of clone type k that were killed by beetles 'this' year.

avstrk: average number of lightning strikes in the stand on a particular day.

avtemp: the simulated 'actual' average temperature on a particular day.

basal: a vector, in which the k-th entry is the total basal area (square feet per acre) of all live trees of clone type k 'this' year.

batch: a variable which has the value zero (0) when the source code is being used to generate the **Interactive** user code, and the value one (1) when generating the **Multiple-Simulation** code.

beetles: a logical variable which is true if there are SPB in the stand, and false otherwise.

beta: second parameter of a gamma distribution for resin flow that is correlated with a previously generated **g0** value (see **alpha**).

betares: second parameter of the gamma distribution for tree resin flow rates reported in Roberds and others (2003) (see **alphares**).

bole: a matrix, in which the i,j entry is the total bole surface area (square feet) of the tree in the i,j position in the stand.

bspc: in simulated stands involving clonal blocks, **bspc** is the number of columns of blocks in the stand.

bspr: in simulated stands involving clonal blocks, **bspr** is the number of rows of blocks in the stand.

cenG0MEAN: the mean of the censored normal distribution from which clonal **g0** values are obtained.

cenG0VAR: the variance of the censored normal distribution from which clonal g0 values are obtained.

cip: a matrix, the i,j entry of which is the 'pine competition index' associated with the tree in the i-th row and j-th column of the stand (see Burkhart and others 1987).

clonetyp: a matrix, in which the i,j entry is the clone number of the tree in the i-th row and the j-th column of the stand (the value is always zero if clones are not used to plant the stand).

clotyp: a matrix, in which the i,j entry is the number of the clone in the clonal block located at the intersection of the i-th row of blocks and the j-th column of blocks in the stand (the value is always zero if clones are not used to plant the stand; if there are clones, but no blocks, then each tree constitutes a 'block').

colda: survival rate (proportion) for landed and parent beetles as a function of low winter temperatures.

coldel: survival rate (proportion) for eggs and larvae as a function of low winter temperatures.

coldp: survival rate (proportion) for pupae as a function of low winter temperatures.

config: The number of the line from the file **configs.txt** that is used in running a particular simulation.

crnlgt: a matrix, in which the i,j entry is the crown length (feet) associated with the tree in the i-th row and j-th column of the stand.

cspb: in simulated stands involving clonal blocks, the number of columns of trees in each block (see **rspb**).

daydied: a matrix, in which the i,j entry is the calendar day (1 = Jan 1, etc.) on which tree i,j died, if it was killed by beetles or by lightning during the course of a simulation. (If it did not die, or if it died because of intra-stand competition, the entry is 0.) This matrix, together with matrix **yrdied**, enables us to track the course of beetle-caused deaths during each stand year, from age 9 until harvest.

depart: a matrix, in which the i,j entry is the total number of beetles leaving tree i,j at the end of one of the four per day update computations.

devpar: a matrix containing parameter values from Ungerer and others (1999) that govern temperature related rates of beetle oviposition, and of maturation rates in the egg, larval, pupal and teneral adult stages (see **devrat**).

devrat: a matrix containing temperature dependent rates of beetle oviposition, and of maturation rates in the egg, larval, pupal and teneral adult stages (see **devpar**).

DFLY: probability of beetle survival during dispersal—depends on temperature.

diam: a matrix, in which the i,j entry is the bole diameter (inches) of the tree in the i,j position in the stand.

diff: in the censored normal distribution used for clonal **g0** (tree growth) rates, the difference between the smallest acceptable **g0** and the mean value of the original distribution. See **ming0**.

distan: In **PTAEDA2** (Burkhart and others 1987), the distance between two competing trees.

dvelop: A vector, the k-th entry of which corresponds to the k-th juvenile life stage (egg, larva, pupa, teneral adult) and represents the proportion of total development within that stage accrued by juveniles in each cohort that is currently in that stage.

dvjuv2: A 3-D array which, together with arrays **mjuv1** and **njuv3**, contains information relating to all juvenile beetles in the stand. The i,j,k entry of dvjuv2 is the proportion of total development within its current developmental class attained thus far by the juvenile cohort oviposited k days earlier in tree(i,j).

eggpro: The temperature dependent proportion of her total complement of eggs that each female parent adult produces on a particular day. Used to calculate both the number of eggs each female parent oviposits on a particular day, and, following Coulson and others (1978) and Gagne and others (1982), the number of female parent beetles that reemerge that day.

factor: A variable that depends on stand age—for each surviving tree in the stand at the beginning of 'this' year, the code computes its current maximum resin flow rate as RMAX = factor*r0 (**r0** is the rate at time of stand planting).

fallen: A numerical constant having value -1. Used in the code to indicate a tree that has been dead at least 5 years.

flow: For each tree, a temporary variable equal to today's total amount of resin lost through beetle attack holes.

g0: A matrix, the i,j entry of which is the overall growth rate of the tree in the i-th row and j-th column of the simulated stand. ('Overall' rate = genotypic rate, plus an added value that represents environmental effects associated with position i,j in the stand and which may be positive or negative.)

g0gain: The difference between the mean of the censored normal distribution used for clonal **g0** (tree growth) rates, and the mean of the original normal distribution.

G0MEAN: The mean of the normal distribution that is sampled to obtain tree growth rates when a stand is planted with improved tree materials. When clonal ramets are used in stand planting, this same distribution is sampled and the values censored to generate the clonal **g0** values (see **gc**).

G0VAR: The variance of the underlying normal distribution that is sampled to obtain tree growth rates (see **G0MEAN**).

gc: A matrix, in which the i,j entry is the genotypic component of the growth rate for the clone planted in the clonal block located at the intersection of the i-th row of blocks and the j-th column of blocks in the stand (see **rc**).

gengam: Random deviate from a gamma distribution having specified alpha and beta parameter values.

gennor: Random deviate from a normal distribution having specified mean and variance.

genunf: Random deviate from a uniform distribution on a specified interval.

gp: A temporary variable used in subroutine **DEPLOY** to fill a clonal block with trees that all have the same genotypic value of growth rate **g0**.

hd: A matrix, in which the entries are computed initially in subroutine **JUVEN**. At the beginning of each subsequent year, the preceding year's values are used in **GROW2** to calculate the new height increments for all surviving trees, after which **hd** is updated for use in the following year.

height: A matrix, in which the i,j entry is the current height of tree(i,j).

hsqg0: The heritability (broad-sense) associated with tree growth rates. (Used in computing the entries in matrix **g0**).

hsqr0: The heritability (broad-sense) associated with tree resin flow rates.

ignbin: Random deviate from a binomial distribution having specified number of 'trials' and 'success' probability.

ignpoi: Random deviate from a Poisson distribution having a specified mean.

immi: A 'character' used in Interactive simulations to indicate on the screen whether there is immigration in each particular year. (immi = 'true' if there is immigration 'that' year, and immi = 'false' if no immigration occurs that year).

killb: A vector, the k-th entry of which counts, for any particular year, the number of trees of clone number k killed by beetles that year.

killc: A vector, the k-th entry of which counts, for any particular year, the number of trees of clone number k killed by competition that year.

killl: A vector, the k-th entry of which counts, for any particular year, the number of trees of clone number k killed by lightning that year.

landed: A matrix, in which the i,j entry is the current number of beetles on the bole surface of tree(i,j). Recomputed four times per simulated day.

light: A matrix, in which the i,j entry is the current number of days since tree(i,j) was struck by lightning (the value = zero if the tree has never been struck).

lowtemp1: A variable equal to the lowest temperature encountered so far in a particular year. Reset to zero at the beginning of each year, then updated daily within the year.

lowtemp2: A variable equal to the second lowest temperature encountered so far in a particular year. Reset to zero at the beginning of each year, then updated daily.

lowtemp3: A variable equal to the third lowest temperature encountered so far in a particular year. Reset to zero at the beginning of each year, then updated daily.

maxday: A numerical constant equal to 469, and representing the last day in a simulated model year (see **minday**).

merch: A vector, the k-th entry of which is the total merchantable timber volume (cubic feet per acre) in surviving trees of clone type k (see **vmerch**).

minday: A numerical constant representing the first day in a simulated model year. Set equal to 105 in order to begin the 'season' after the last cold winter temperatures (value will change depending on the geographical location of the stand being simulated—see **maxday**).

ming0: In the censored normal distribution used for clonal **g0** (tree growth) rates, the smallest acceptable **g0** value.

mjuv1: A 3-D array which, together with arrays **dvjuv2** and **njuv3**, contains information relating to all juvenile beetles in the stand. The i,j,k entry of mjuv1 is the current developmental class (egg, larva, pupa or teneral adult) attained by the juvenile cohort oviposited k days earlier in tree(i,j).

mtemp: Average temperature during a 3-hour update period.

mu: The mean value of the normal random variable representing the number of successful beetle penetrations per square meter of bole area required to kill a tree (see **sig**).

nalive: The current total number of live trees in the stand.

natk: A matrix, in which the i,j entry is the cumulative number of beetle attacks on tree(i,j) during a day.

nc: The number of columns of trees in the simulated stand. This parameter is read in **MAIN** from an input file.

nc0: Temporary value of **nc**.

nclone: A vector, the k-th entry of which is the total number of trees of clone type k planted in the stand.

nday: During a simulation, **nday** is the current day of the year for which computations are being made.

ndead: The total number of dead trees in the stand.

nemrge: A temporary variable equal to the number of juveniles that mature and emerge from a particular tree 'today.' Added to the departing group of beetles prior to daily dispersal.

nenter: A matrix, the i,j entry of which is the cumulative number of successful beetle penetrations 'today.'

newegg: For each tree(i,j) in the code computations, the name used temporarily for the total number of eggs oviposited in that tree on a particular day. The value is later stored as the i,j,1 entry in the 3-D array **njuv3**.

newneg: A matrix, the i,j entry of which is the current repelling (male) pheromone concentration currently being generated in tree(i,j).

newpos: A matrix, the i,j entry of which is the current attracting (female) pheromone concentration currently being generated on and/or in tree(i,j).

nfallen: In a simulation, the cumulative number of 'fallen' trees (trees that died 5 or more years ago) in the stand.

nimmi: A variable which equals zero if there is no beetle migration into the stand 'this' year, and equals 1 if there is migration.

njuv3: A 3-D array which, together with arrays **mjuv1** and **dvjuv2**, contains information relating to all juvenile beetles in the stand. The i,j,k entry of **njuv3** is the number of survivors in the juvenile cohort resulting from oviposition k days earlier in tree(i,j).

nmale: The current number of male SPB in a tree. Used only to compute the current concentration of male, repelling pheromone being produced.

nnpen: A matrix, in which the i,j entry is the cumulative number of beetle penetrations in tree(i,j) so far this year, as of the beginning of 'today.' Used to compute the probability tree(i,j) dies from beetle penetrations today. See **npen**.

npen: A matrix, in which the i,j entry is the cumulative number of beetle penetrations in tree(i,j) so far this year, by today's end. Used to compute the probability that tree(i,j) dies from beetle penetrations today. See **nnpen**.

nr: The number of rows of trees in the stand. This parameter is read in **MAIN** from an input file.

nr0: Temporary value of **nr**, the total number of rows in the stand.

nreemr: A temporary variable whose value is the number parent beetles that reemerge from a particular tree 'today.'

nsim: The number of the simulation currently being processed, when running a group of simulations chosen from the list **input.txt**.

nstay: A temporary variable whose value is the number of parent beetles that do not reemerge from a particular tree 'today' (i.e., remain in the tree at day's end).

nstrks: The number of lightning strikes in the stand today (a Poisson deviate).

ntrees: The total number of trees planted in a simulated stand (equal to nr*nc).

numcln: In simulations involving clones, the number of clones used in planting the stand.

numdevs: A parameter: In the censored normal distribution used for clonal **g0** (tree growth) rates, the number of standard deviations between the mean value of the original distribution and the smallest acceptable value of **g0**. See **diff** and **ming0**.

numtre: A variable, the value of which is the total number of live trees in a simulated stand at the beginning of 'this year.'

nyears: The harvest age (at least 9 years but otherwise unrestricted) of a simulated stand.

oalive: A numerical constant having value +2. Used in the code to indicate a tree that is currently still alive.

odead: A numerical constant having value zero. Used in the code to indicate a tree that died, due to beetle attacks, lightning or intrastand competition.

paremi: A parameter whose value is used to calibrate the probability that a particular beetle emigrates from the stand during a particular update period.

parent: A matrix, the i,j entry of which is the current number of ovipositing adult females in tree(i,j).

parimmi: A parameter, used to calibrate the number of beetles that migrate into a stand during an update period.

phrmax: A temporary variable, whose value is the highest positive pheromone concentration among the 9 trees located no more than one row or column away from a particular tree of interest.

phrneg: A matrix, the i,j entry of which is the present concentration of repelling (male) pheromone (from all sources) surrounding tree(i,j).

phrpos: A matrix, the i,j entry of which is the present concentration of attracting (female) pheromone (from all sources) surrounding tree(i,j).

PI: A constant, the value of which is 3.141592653585.

pra: A temporary variable, used in computing the probability a particular tree dies from beetle penetrations 'today.'

prb: Another temporary variable, used in computing the probability a particular tree dies from beetle penetrations 'today.'

premi: For each individual 'dispersing' beetle, the current probability that it migrates out of the stand during an update period.

propor: The proportion of beetle attacks on a tree that lead to successful penetration.

px: The distance (feet) between adjacent columns in a simulated stand.

px0: The assigned value of variable **px**: read from an input file at the beginning of a simulation.

py: The distance (feet) between adjacent rows in a simulated stand.

py0: The assigned value of variable **py**: read from an input file at the beginning of a simulation.

qblock: A parameter, equal to 1 if a simulated stand involves clonal blocks, and 2 if there are no blocks.

qclone: A parameter, equal to 1 if a simulated stand involves clones, and zero if there are no clones.

qimmi: A logical variable, equal to 1 if there is beetle migration into the stand 'this' year, and zero if there is no immigration this year.

qspb: A logical parameter, equal to 1 if a simulated stand involves beetles, and zero if there are no beetles.

r0: A matrix, the i,j entry of which is the overall resin flow rate of the tree in the i-th row and j-th column of the simulated stand. ('Overall' rate = genotypic rate, plus an added value that represents environmental effects associated with position i,j in the stand and which may be positive or negative.)

r0g0mean: The 'correlated mean' of resin flow rate **r0**, given a previously determined value of tree growth rate **g0**.

r0g0var: The 'correlated variance' of resin flow rate **r0**, given a previously determined value of tree growth rate **g0**.

r0mean: The mean of the underlying distribution from which simulated resin flows are randomly generated (see Roberds and others 2003).

r0var: The variance of the underlying distribution from which simulated resin flows are randomly generated (see **r0mean**).

RATK3: A parameter that relates to the relative decrease in rate of transition of landed beetles (see **landed**) to the attacking stage, per unit increase in **phrneg** (repelling pheromone).

ratk50: A parameter, used to calibrate the proportion of beetle attacks that result in successful penetration of a tree.

RATK6: A parameter that relates to the relative increase in rate of transition of landed beetles (see **landed**) to the attacking stage, per unit increase in **phrpos** (attracting pheromone level).

rbeg: The first line chosen from file **input.txt** when simulating a 'batch' of stands (see chapter IV of this documentation—also see **rend**).

rc: A matrix, the i,j entry of which is the genotypic component of the resin flow rate associated with the clone planted in the clonal block located at the intersection of the i-th row of blocks and the j-th column of blocks in the stand (see **gc**).

rend: The last line chosen from file **input.txt** when simulating a 'batch' of stands (see chapter IV of this documentation—also see **rbeg**).

resin: A matrix, the i,j entry of which is the basic resin level for tree(i,j), expressed as flow per day (g), per currently open beetle penetration hole. In model simulations, holes remain open for only one day.

rho: The coefficient of correlation between same-tree values of the tree growth rate **g0** and the tree resin flow rate **r0**.

RMAX: A matrix, the i,j entry of which is the maximum resin flow rate, at the present stand age, of the tree in the i-th row and j-th column of the stand. Based on Roberds and others (2003).

rp: A temporary variable used to fill a clonal block with trees which all have the same genotypic value of resin flow rate **r0**.

RPHER1: A constant, the value of which is the increase in concentration of positive pheromone (see **newpos**) around a tree, per successfully attacking female.

RPHER2: A constant, the value of which is the increase in concentration of negative pheromone (see **newneg**) being produced in a tree, per male consort of a female that has successfully penetrated the tree.

rspb: In simulated stands involving clonal blocks, the number of rows of trees in each block (see **cspb**).

savdiam: Average diameter (inches) of all live trees 'this' year.

savdiamkb: Average diameter (inches) of all trees that were killed by beetles 'this' year.

savdiamkc: Average diameter (inches) of all trees that were killed by competition 'this' year.

savhgt: Average height (feet) of all live trees 'this' year.

savhgtkb: Average height (feet) of all trees that were killed by beetles 'this' year.

savhgtkc: Average height (feet) of all trees that were killed by competition 'this' year.

savres: Average resin flow rate (g/24h) of all live trees 'this' year.

savreskb: Average resin flow rate (g/24h) of all trees that were killed by beetles 'this' year.

sbasal: Total basal area (square feet per acre) of all live trees in the stand 'this' year.

seed: The number of the line from the file **input.txt** that is used to initiate a particular simulation.

seed1: In model simulations, two seeds are used to generate random values associated with temperature, trees and beetles, so these quantities can be randomized within and between simulations.

seed2: See **seed1**.

sig: The standard deviation of the normal random variable representing the number of successful beetle penetrations per square meter of bole area required to kill a tree (see **mu**).

sim: A temporary variable, the value of which is the current simulation (line number in the file input.txt) in a batch sequence of simulations.

siteg0: The environmental value added to a tree's genotypic **g0**-value during the planting process.

siter0: The environmental value added to a tree's genotypic **r0**-value during the planting process.

sjuv: The probability of juvenile survival on a particular day, as a function of the amount of maturation on that day.

skillb: A variable which, for any particular year, counts the total number of trees in the stand killed by beetles that year.

skillc: A variable which, for any particular year, counts the total number of trees in the stand killed by competition that year.

skilll: A variable which, for any particular year, counts the total number of trees in the stand killed by lightning that year.

smerch: The total volume (cubic feet per acre) of merchantable timber in surviving trees in the stand (see **vmerch**).

ssurv: A variable which, for any particular year, counts the total number of surviving trees in the stand at the end of that year.

staytokill: A logical variable which, if equal to 'true', indicates that beetles don't leave when tree death is imminent. In this circumstance, the proportion of landed beetles that attack on a particular day equals the ratio of variable **npen** to the 'expected' total number of beetle penetrations that will ultimately be required to kill the tree.

surv: A vector, the k-th element of which is the number of surviving ramets of clone k.

surv1: The probability that a juvenile beetle is alive at the beginning of a day, as a function of its level of maturation.

surv2: The probability that a juvenile beetle is alive at the end of a day, as a function of its level of maturation.

survd: The probability that a beetle departing from one tree survives to land on another, not necessarily different, tree in the stand.

survp: The probability that a parent beetle survives throughout a particular day, as a function of the proportion of her total egg production deposited that day.

t0: A matrix, the i,j entry of which is the resin toxicity of the tree in the i-th row and j-th column of the stand. This parameter is not used in current (November 2007) source code computations.

T0MEAN: The mean value of the resin toxicity distribution. Not used in current (November 2007) source code computations.

T0VAR: The variance of the resin toxicity distribution. Not used in current (November 2007) source code computations.

TAMPL: In model simulations, the amplitude of the maximum deviation of daily average temperature from the yearly mean. Computed as July average minus **TMEAN**.

tavg: Long-term average temperature on a particular day.

TC: A matrix, the i,j entry of which is the genotypic value of the resin toxicity of the clone planted in the clonal block located in the i-th row and j-th column of blocks in the stand. Not used in current (November 2007) source code computations.

tdev: Simulated maximum temperature deviation away from the simulated average for a particular day.

tdmean: Mean of **tdev**—this varies over the year.

TDVAR: The variance of **tdev** around its mean, **tdmean**.

THRESH: Temperature threshold (°C) below which no beetle activity occurs, except possible mortality, and no degree-days are accumulated.

tmax: The simulated highest temperature (°C) on a particular day.

TMEAN: The long-term yearly mean average temperature (°C). A major input parameter.

tmerch: The total volume (cubic feet per acre) of merchantable timber in the stand.

tmin: The simulated lowest temperature on a particular day.

totegg: The total number of SPB eggs deposited in a particular tree on a particular day.

tp: The number of trees planted per acre.

tree: A matrix, in which the i,j entry indicates the current status of the tree in the i,j position of the stand:

tree(i,j) = 2 if the tree is alive
= 0 if the tree died in a preceding year or died from competition this year
= -1 if the tree is 'fallen' (i.e., died over 5 years ago and is no longer standing)

TVAR: The variance of **avtemp** around its mean, **tavg**.

urand: Random deviate from a uniform distribution on the interval [0,1].

vmerch: A matrix, the i,j entry of which is the current number of cubic feet of merchantable timber in tree(i,j) (adapted from **PTAEDA2**—Burkhart and others 1987). Only live trees have positive **vmerch**.

voldbh: Minimum d.b.h. (inches) considered in merchantable volume computation (see **PTAEDA2**—Burkhart and others 1987).

voltop: Minimum upper bole diameter (inches) included in merchantable volume computation (see **PTAEDA2**—Burkhart and others 1987).

voltyp: Indicates the type of merchantable volume reported (see **PTAEDA2**—Burkhart and others 1987). In **SPBLOB**, volume is 'inside bark.'

xbeg: Maturity level (cumulative) of a juvenile cohort at the beginning of a simulated day.

xcoord: A matrix, in which the i,j entry indicates the horizontal distance (in feet) between tree(i,j) and the upper left corner of the stand.

xend: Maturity level (cumulative) of a juvenile cohort at the end of a simulated day.

xxxjuv: Average number of juvenile beetles, per attacked tree.

xxxland: Average number of landed beetles, per attacked tree.

xxxpar: Average number of parent beetles, per attacked tree.

ycoord: A matrix, in which the i,j entry indicates the vertical distance (in feet) between tree(i,j) and the upper left corner of the stand.

yrdied: A matrix, in which the i,j entry indicates the stand year in which tree(i,j) died. This entry is 0 if the tree lives until harvest. (Trees that die during the juvenile phase are assigned value 8.) This matrix, together with matrix **daydied**, enables us to track the course of beetle-caused deaths throughout the life of the stand, from planting until harvest.

yrnum: A variable whose value is the current stand age in a simulation.

APPENDIX A—DOWNLOADING, INSTALLING, AND USING THE OPENWATCOM COMPILERS

A. Download and Installation

Users running Windows or OS/2 systems can download this compiler from **http://www.openwatcom.org/**

The current (November 2007) version is 1.7a, released in October, 2007. There are two installation files, one for C/C++ and the other for FORTRAN. Once you have opened this web site you can:

(1) Go to the section headed "Latest release" and find "as well as the release source archive is available for download." The word "download" is a link; click on it.

(2) In the page called "Open Watcom 1.7a", look for the first mirror and "Installers (Windows, OS/2)." Click the "HTTP" link.

(3) To download, click the files named "open-watcom-c-win32-1.7a.exe" and "open-watcom-f77-win32-1.7a.exe."

To install the files, find the downloaded files, click on them one at a time and follow the instructions on the screen. You will need to install the two files consecutively in your 'Programs' folder, first the 'C' file, then the 'fortran' file. (We used both C codes and FORTRAN codes in **SPBLOB**, and some of the FORTRAN subroutines depend on random number generators written in C. Details are in chapter V and appendix B.)

B. Compiling a Modified SPBLOB Source code

After installation of both files, go to 'Start->Programs->Open Watcom FORTRAN.' In the resulting menu, click 'IDE.' The Open Watcom IDE (Integrated Development Environment) will begin running and you will see this window:

Click on 'File', then on 'Open Project.'

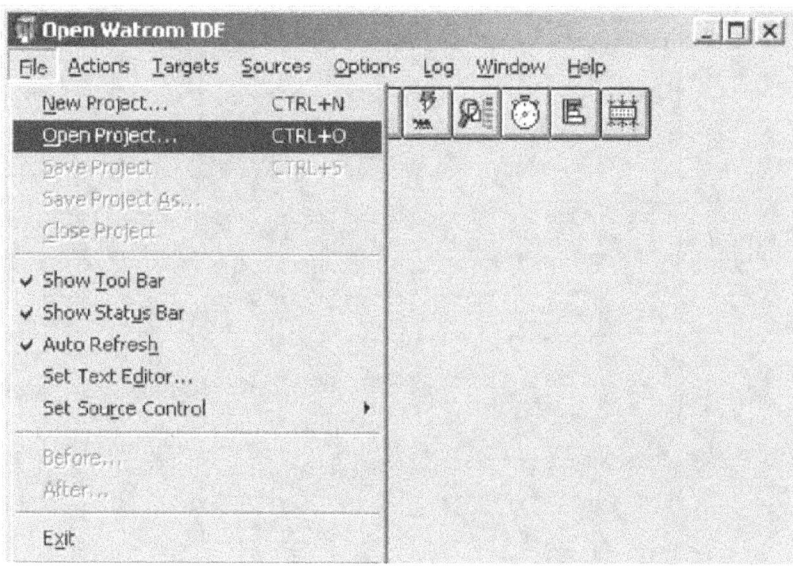

Browse to the folder where your downloaded source code resides, and open the project file it contains by typing **tree.wpj** in the 'File_name' box at the bottom of the window and then click on 'Open.'

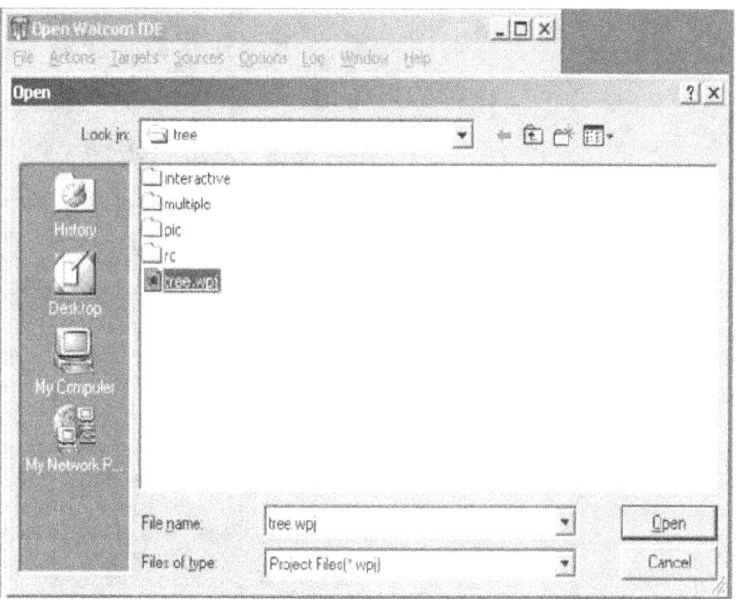

You will see a screen listing three 'Source files.'

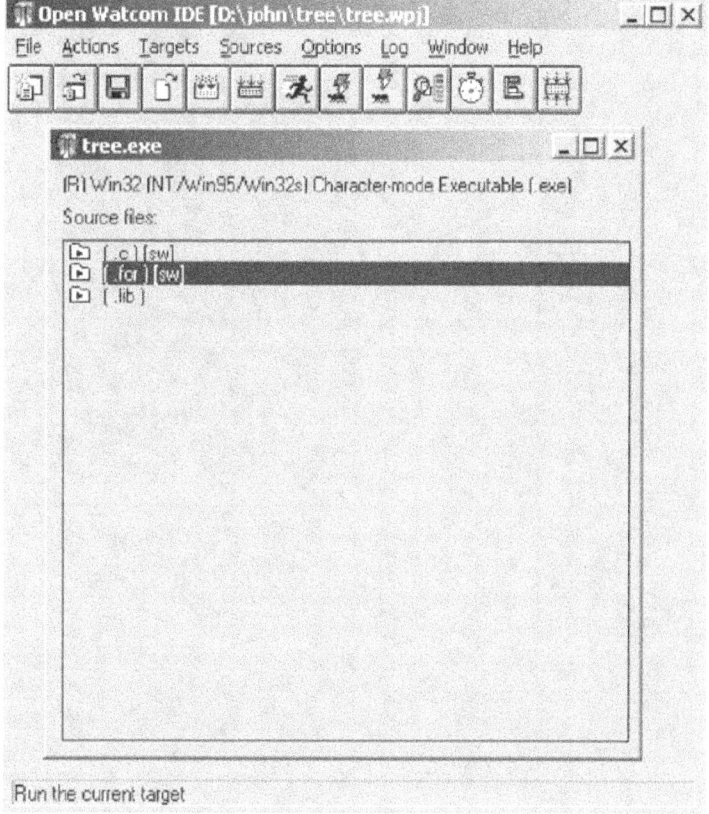

Here, you can click, e.g., on the second icon to branch out the source code files.

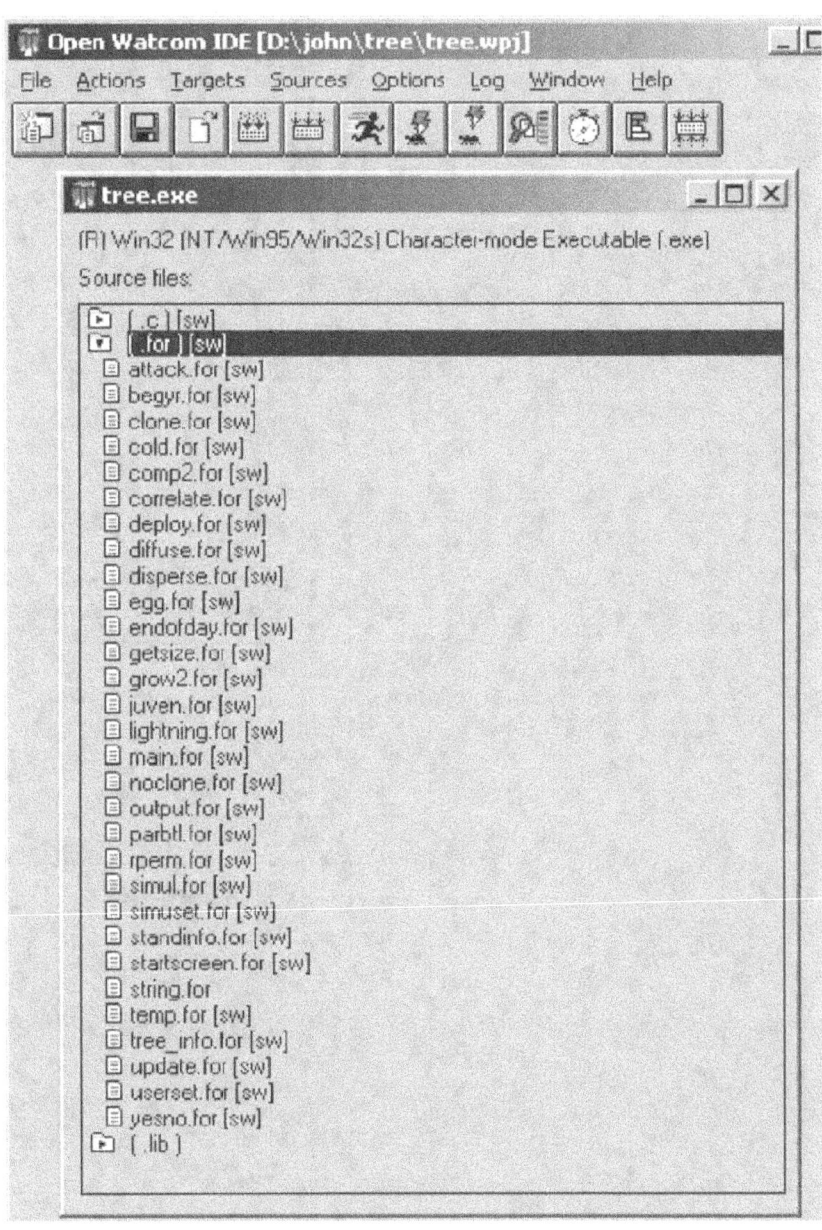

Now you can check or modify the code subroutines. As an example, if you want to change **main.for**, double click **main.for** in the list of subroutines. This brings up the editor window with **main.for** opened (Note: details displayed may be different if you have a newer version of **SPBLOB**).

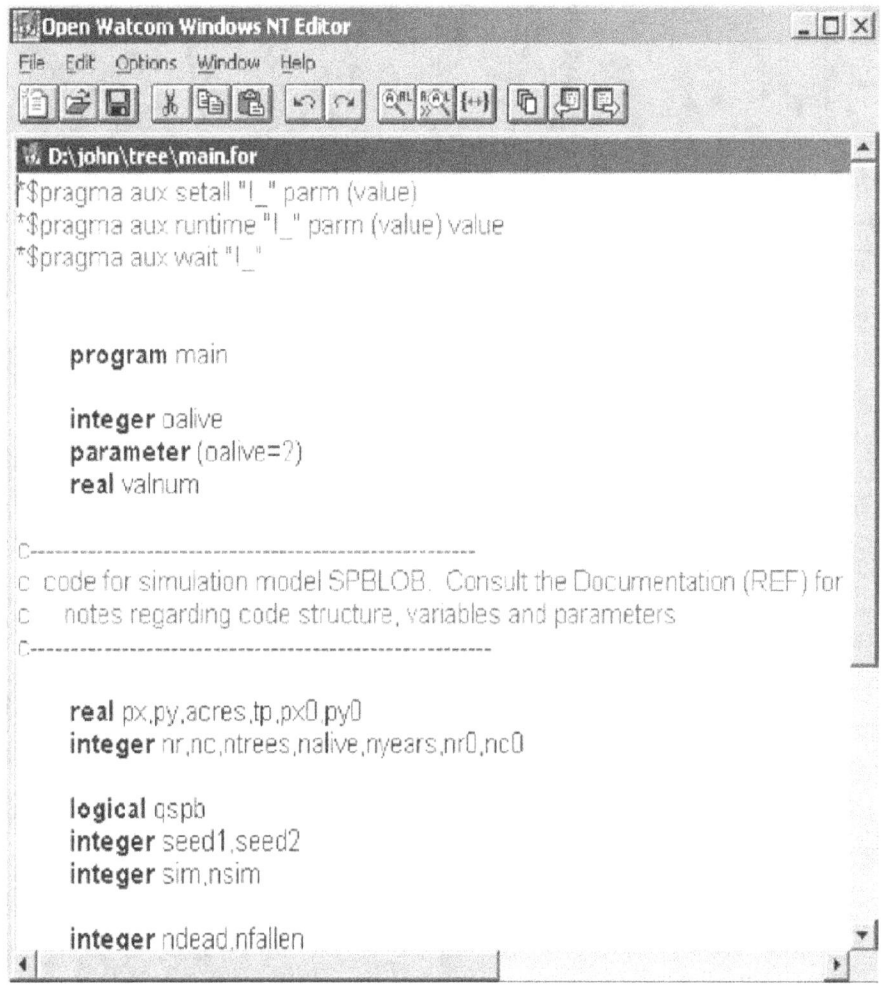

After making your desired modifications, save the changes by clicking the 'save' icon, or clicking 'File', then 'Save' in the menu at the top. Then follow the same procedure to edit other subroutines, as desired. Once your modifications are complete, return to the IDE window and on the menu, click 'Targets' and 'Make.'

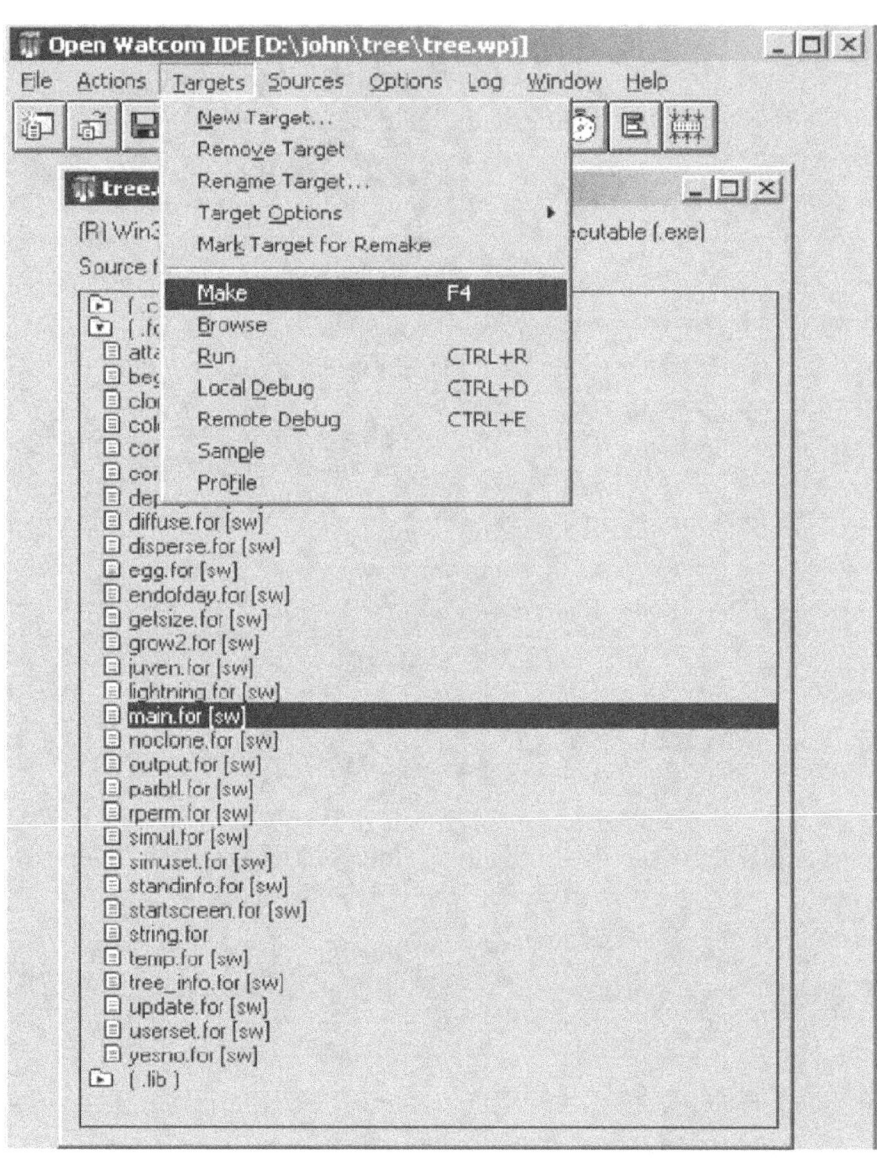

If there are no errors in the modified code, an updated executable file **tree.exe** is now ready for use. Any errors will be indicated in the 'IDE Log' that appears at the bottom of the IDE window. Correct these errors as described, then repeat the 'Targets -> Make' process.

Reminder from **chapter V**—The **Interactive** and **Multiple-Simulation** versions of the code share the same set of source files. To alter and re-compile the **Interactive** version, make sure the parameter **batch** in **main.for** is set equal to zero before re-compiling, as in this screen.

To recompile the **Multiple Simulations** version, make sure **batch=1** in **main.for**.

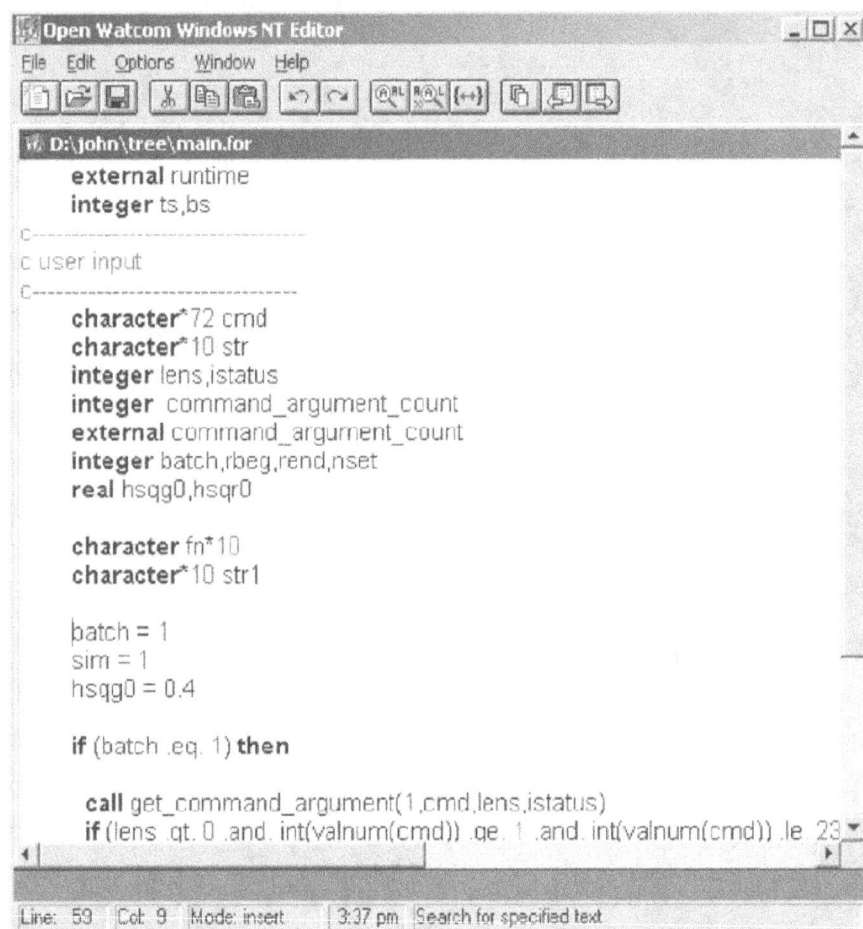

Once the modified code is successfully re-compiled, you can run it in the usual way, as described in **chapter V**.

Important: If you recompile the **Interactive** version of the code, you must insert the resulting new executable **tree** file into the **interactive** folder in place of the old one before running new simulations. Similarly, after recompiling the **Multiple** version, insert the resulting executable **tree** file into the **multiple** folder, then run your new simulations.

Note: Detailed usage of the **Open Watcom** compiler system can be found in its help files, Web site, and newsgroups.

APPENDIX B—LEGALITIES

A. Introduction

The compilers, random number generators, and command files used in connection with the **SPBLOB** code have been downloaded from sites in the public domain. Some citations and credits appear in **chapter V** of this documentation. This appendix contains detailed information concerning disclaimers and legal requirements associated with these uses, and also with the use of the **SPBLOB** model and code. Briefly, we place the model and code in the public domain. However, some of the code related to random number generation originates in Association for Computing Machinery (ACM) publications. ACM retains copyright to this code, but allows use in any computer for any purpose, with the restriction that distribution for commercial purposes requires permission from the ACM, and perhaps payment.

B. Web Sources

Technical material downloaded for use with the **SPBLOB** code originates from three Web sites:

- Subroutines **'get_command_argument'** and **'command_argument_count'** from the lib file **f2kcli.lib**

  http://www.winteracter.com/f2kcli

- **OpenWatcom** Fortran and C code compilers from **SYBASE, INC**

  http://www.openwatcom.org

- Code files for random number generators (**RANDLIB**) from the **Software Download Site of the Department of Biostatistics & Applied Mathematics of the University of Texas M.D. Anderson Cancer Center**

  http://biostatistics.mdanderson.org/SoftwareDownload/SingleSoftware. aspx?Software_Id=27

C. Legalities
C.1. f2kcli

While no legal statement is required by **Interactive Software Services Limited**, we wish to acknowledge with thanks our use of their **f2kcli** command line interface.

C.2. SYBASE, INC.

OpenWatcom Fortran and C code compilers have been used in compliance with the **Sybase Open Watcom Public License version 1.0** to compile our source code and produce the executable **Interactive** and **Multiple Simulation** files included in the **SPBLOB** code folder **spblob_11_27_2007**.

C.3. RANDLIB

C.3.1 From the RANDLIB90 README FILE
RANDLIB90 is a set of Fortran 90 routines that generate random numbers from the usual statistical distributions. The complete description of functionality is found in the documentation files.

=========================FILES============================
The following files should be present when you unpack this code.

INSTALLATION: Instructions on compiling and installing the code. The instructions are necessarily vague because almost any computer with any operating system could contain these programs.

LEGALITIES: Describes the legalities of use of the code. Briefly: We place our efforts in the public domain, but much of the code originates from ACM publications. ACM retains copyright to this code but allows the use in any computer for any purpose. However, distribution for commercial gain requires permission from the ACM and perhaps payment.

C.3.2 The RANDLIB90 LEGALITIES FILE

Legalities

We place our efforts in writing this package in the public domain. However, code from ACM publications is subject to the ACM policy.

References

Base Generator:
The base generator and all code in the ecuyer_cote_mod come from the reference **P. L'Ecuyer and S. Cote.** (1991) "Implementing a Random Number Package with Splitting Facilities." ACM Trans. on Math. Softw. 17:1, pp 98-111. We transliterated the Pascal of the reference to Fortran 95.

The Beta Random Number Generator:
R. C. H. Cheng (1978) "Generating Beta Variates with Nonintegral Shape Parameters." Communications of the ACM, 21:317-322. (Algorithms B and BC)

The Binomial Random Number Generator:
Kachitvichyanukul, V. and Schmeiser, B. W. (1988) "Binomial Random Variate Generation." Communications of the ACM, 31: 216. (Algorithm BTPE.)

The Standard Exponential Random Number Generator:
Ahrens, J.H. and Dieter, U. (1972) "Computer Methods for Sampling from the Exponential and Normal Distributions." Communications of the ACM, 15: 873-882. (Algorithm SA.)

The Standard Gamma Random Number Generator:
Ahrens, J.H. and Dieter, U. (1982) "Generating Gamma Variates by a Modified Rejection Technique." Communications of the ACM, 25: 47-54. (Algorithm SA.)

The Standard Normal Random Number Generator:
Ahrens, J.H. and Dieter, U. (1973) "Extensions of Forsythe's Method for Random Sampling from the Normal Distribution." Math. Comput. 27: 927-937. (Algorithm FL, method=5)

ACM Policy on Use of Code
Here is the software Policy of the ACM:

Submittal of an algorithm for publication in one of the ACM transactions implies that unrestricted use of the algorithm within a computer is permissible. General permission to copy and distribute the algorithm without fee is granted provided that the copies are not made or distributed for direct commercial advantage. The ACM copyright notice and the title of the publication and its date appear, and notice is given that copying is by permission of the Association for Computing Machinery. To copy otherwise, or to republish, requires a fee and/or specific permission. Krogh, F. (1997) "Algorithms Policy." ACM Tran. Math. Softw. 13, 183-186. We do not know the policy of the Royal Statistical Society; they have discontinued publishing algorithms. However, they made a number of these programs available on Statlib on condition that there be no charge for their distribution.

Here is our standard disclaimer:

NO WARRANTY

WE PROVIDE ABSOLUTELY NO WARRANTY OF ANY KIND EITHER EXPRESSED OR IMPLIED, INCLUDING BUT NOT LIMITED TO, THE IMPLIED WARRANTIES OF MERCHANTABILITY AND FITNESS FOR A PARTICULAR PURPOSE. THE ENTIRE RISK AS TO THE QUALITY AND PERFORMANCE OF THE PROGRAM IS WITH YOU. SHOULD THIS PROGRAM PROVE DEFECTIVE, YOU ASSUME THE COST OF ALL NECESSARY SERVICING, REPAIR OR CORRECTION. IN NO EVENT SHALL THE UNIVERSITY OF TEXAS OR ANY OF ITS COMPONENT INSTITUTIONS INCLUDING M. D. ANDERSON HOSPITAL BE LIABLE TO YOU FOR DAMAGES, INCLUDING ANY LOST PROFITS, LOST MONIES, OR OTHER SPECIAL, INCIDENTAL OR CONSEQUENTIAL DAMAGES ARISING OUT OF THE USE OR INABILITY TO USE (INCLUDING BUT NOT LIMITED TO LOSS OF DATA OR ITS ANALYSIS BEING RENDERED INACCURATE OR LOSSES SUSTAINED BY THIRD PARTIES) THE PROGRAM.

(Above NO WARRANTY modified from the GNU NO WARRANTY statement.)

www.ingramcontent.com/pod-product-compliance
Lightning Source LLC
Chambersburg PA
CBHW081228280526
45787CB00006B/2569